# TOMY LESSO

## THE GREAT FAMILY OF VISCERA

Offal - or 'organ meats' - represents the family of edible animal innards.

It's a very broad family, both in the diversity of its members and their textures. It's a long way from the foot to the cheek. So there's something for every taste and also for every budget ('fries' are very cheap!)...

Expensive sweetbreads will play the star over cheap tripe.

### POULTRY

**A** GIZZARD
**B** HEART
**C** LIVER

been reached on a classification system. Below is the one used in this book:

#### WHITE OFFAL

feet, brains, spinal cord, tripe, head, ears, teat (udder)

#### RED OFFAL

lungs, heart, liver, kidneys, fries (testicles), tail, cheeks, tongue, snout, sweetbreads, skirt steak and hanger steak.

Other items such as the pope's eye (or 'spider' steak) and marrow bones complete this great family.

### SHEEP (OR LAMB)

**A** TONGUE
**B** BRAIN
**C** THYMUS GLAND (SWEETBREADS)
**D** HEART
**E** SPINAL CORD
**F** KIDNEYS
**G** TRIPE
**H** FRIES
**I** FEET

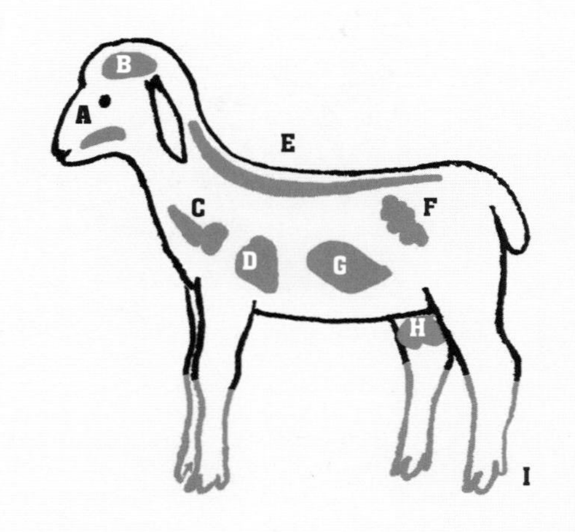


### PIG

**A** HEAD
**B** BRAIN
**C** TONGUE
**D** CHEEK
**E** HEART
**F** LIVER
**G** KIDNEYS
**H** INTESTINES
**I** TAIL
**J** FEET

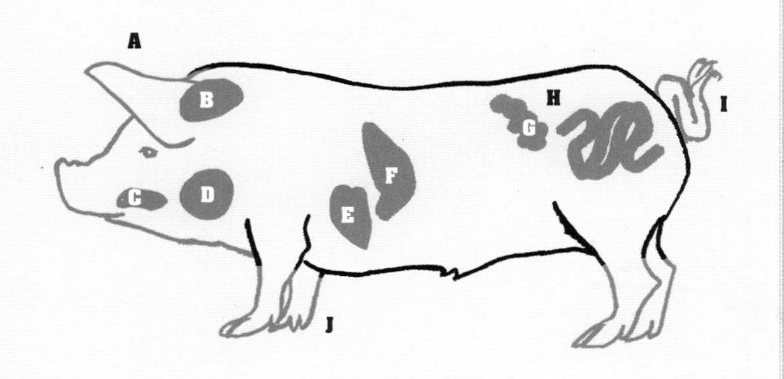

# STÉPHANE REYNAUD'S

# BOOK OF TRIPE

A big thank you to Marie-Pierre – what do you know, I seem to be missing a brain today – and to José, always on top of his game.
Thank you, Pauline for this very good trip.
Thank you, Ciinniinniiii.
Thank you, Aurélie, the unknown lady of the emails, and your typo-hunting.
Thank you, Jacquy, it had been a while.

First published by Marabout in 2012.

Published in 2014 by Murdoch Books, an imprint of Allen & Unwin.

Murdoch Books Australia
83 Alexander Street
Crows Nest NSW 2065
Phone: +61 (0) 2 8425 0100
Fax: +61 (0) 2 9906 2218
www.murdochbooks.com.au
info@murdochbooks.com.au

Murdoch Books UK
Erico House, 6th Floor
93–99 Upper Richmond Road
Putney, London SW15 2TG
Phone: +44 (0) 20 8785 5995
Fax: +44 (0) 20 8785 5985
www.murdochbooks.co.uk
info@murdochbooks.co.uk

For Corporate Orders & Custom Publishing contact
Noel Hammond, National Business Development Manager, Murdoch Books Australia

Publisher: Sue Hines
Photographer: Marie-Pierre Morel
Stylist: Élodie Rambaud
Illustrations: José Reis De Matos
Translator: Melissa McMahon
Editor: Katie Bosher
Food editor and testing: Sonja Bernyk
Project editor: Claire Grady
Production: Karen Small



A cataloguing-in-publication entry is available from the catalogue of the National Library of Australia at www.nla.gov.au.

A catalogue record for this book is available from the British Library.

Colour reproduction by Splitting Image, Clayton, Victoria.

Printed by 1010 Printing.

IMPORTANT: Those who might be at risk from the effects of salmonella poisoning (the elderly, pregnant women, young children and those suffering from immune deficiency diseases) should consult their doctor with any concerns about eating raw eggs.

OVEN GUIDE: You may find cooking times vary depending on the oven you are using. For fan-forced ovens, as a general rule, set the oven temperature to 20°C (35°F) lower than indicated in the recipe.

MEASURES GUIDE: We have used 20 ml (4 teaspoon) tablespoon measures. If you are using a 15 ml (3 teaspoon) tablespoon add an extra teaspoon of the ingredient for each tablespoon specified.

The stylist would like to thank:
Couteau TB: www.tb-groupe.fr
Concrete-wax backdrops Marius Aurenti: www.mariusaurenti.com
Couverts Cutipol: www.cutipol.pt

The food editor would like to thank Phillip Mitchell and his team of butchers from Castlecrag Meats for his assistance, expertise and knowledge in offal and whole beast butchery: www.castlecragmeats.com.au

STÉPHANE REYNAUD'S

# BOOK OF

## and gizzards, kidneys, feet, brains and all the rest

◆ ◆ ◆ ◆

PHOTOGRAPHS

**MARIE-PIERRE MOREL**

ILLUSTRATIONS

**JOSÉ REIS DE MATOS**

MURDOCH BOOKS

# ON THE MENU

# WELCOME TO THE WORLD OF OFFAL

Heart, gizzards, tripe, brains, tail... These pieces that we perhaps wouldn't cook, whether from lack of culinary knowledge or fear, make up the great family of offal. Mamma mia!

They are often reserved for private consumption between friends and enlightened enthusiasts. There is something rather manly or masculine about offal, but look more closely and its feminine side, soft and delicate, is never very far away. Calf's head isn't cooked in one-person serves, it's something you gather around. We cook tripe in batches of at least five kilograms, so we'll keep some in the freezer and set aside a serving or two for the neighbours, who love it but don't dare cook it. A beef cheek bourguignon will be the joy of Sunday lunch and for days afterwards — it is so much better reheated! Forget prejudices, go back to the butcher, get some advice and dare to cook.

Offal appears in daily life in many dishes. A sausage cannot exist without its intestinal casing, andouillette is filled with pig's innards, terrines are often packed with pork liver, with a soft piece of caul fat wrapped around them...

Offal is all around us. It's there, lurking on a friendly butcher's display and waiting patiently for the chance to take centre stage on our plates and shout loud and clear:

## TOUS À TABLE!

# LE FOIE

## LIVER

**BEEF LIVER:** ready to cook (prepared by the butcher)

**CALF'S LIVER:** ready to cook (prepared by the butcher)

**PORK LIVER:** ready to cook (prepared by the butcher. May need to be ordered ahead)

**LAMB'S LIVER:** ready to cook (prepared by the butcher. May need to be ordered ahead)

**CHICKEN (OR OTHER POULTRY) LIVER:** remove the gall bladder (small green pouch) if still attached

## ORGAN LOCATED IN THE ABDOMEN, THAT SECRETES BILE AND WORKS TO METABOLISE CARBOHYDRATES, FATS AND PROTEINS

The liver is a powerhouse of nutrients. High in protein and low in fat, it is the ally of every diet: Are you fat? 'Eat some liver!' Are you skinny? 'Eat some liver!' It is also, however, a catalyst of heavy metals and purines, so keep an eye on your big toe; gout lies in wait for the high livers who overindulge...

In the collective memory, the liver has the peculiar characteristic of being associated with a sort of fertiliser that will help the littlest among us to shoot up like flowers in springtime. 'Don't fret, *mon petit*, eat your liver and you'll grow in no time,' my grandmother would say to me with the benevolence of a loving mamie. It's true that at sixteen years old, 162 centimetres tall and 0.096 tonnes, there was reason to fear that a few psychological complexes lay ahead. But I did not fret, I controlled my bile, my liver took care of it. The growth spurt happened: 25 extra centimetres at the withers for 0.100 tonnes at the weigh-in. Granny's faith in the liver was confirmed, a legend that was to live on.

Since that day, the life of the liver has continued unperturbed, and so much the better. 'Eat your liver, *mes petits*, and you'll grow in no time,' a certain Stéphane was saying the other day, with the benevolence of a loving papa!

# CALF'S LIVER LES HALLES STYLE

**SERVES 6**
**10 MINUTES PREPARATION TIME**
**10 MINUTES COOKING TIME**

6 thick slices of calf's liver (about 750 g/1 lb 10 oz)
35 g (1¼ oz/¼ cup) plain (all-purpose) flour
Salt and pepper
150 g (5½ oz) butter, chopped
4 French shallots, thinly sliced
2 tablespoons raspberry vinegar

**THE LIVER**
Since calf's liver is best eaten pink, it's good to get slices that are thick, rather than wide. Flour and season the liver slices.

**COOKING**
In a large heavy-based frying pan, preferably made of cast iron (it's better), melt the butter over a medium heat until it becomes foamy. Add the shallots and cook, stirring occasionally, for 3 minutes, or until softened. Add the liver to the pan and cook for 2–3 minutes on each side, or until browned but still pink in the centre. Deglaze the pan with the vinegar just before serving.

**SERVE WITH**
A good potato purée sauced with the shallot sauce.

# CALF'S LIVER WITH A HERB CRUST

**SERVES 6**
**45 MINUTES PREPARATION TIME**
**1 HOUR CHILLING TIME**
**20 MINUTES COOKING TIME**

50 g (1¾ oz) stale bread, coarsely chopped
250 g (9 oz/1 cup) butter, softened
1 bunch of parsley, leaves picked
1 bunch of tarragon, leaves picked
1 French shallot, finely chopped
Salt and pepper
700 g (1 lb 9 oz) kipfler (fingerling) potatoes, scrubbed and dried
2 tablespoons olive oil
2 bay leaves
3 garlic cloves
6 bulb spring onions (scallions), trimmed and halved lengthways
100 g (3½ oz) smoked lardons, cut into 1 cm (½ inch) thick strips (see note)
6 thick slices of calf's liver (about 750 g/1 lb 10 oz)

**THE HERB CRUST**

Finely chop the bread,150 g (5½ oz) of the butter and the parsley and tarragon leaves in a food processor to make a good thick paste. Stir in the shallot by hand and season with salt and pepper. Roll out the herb paste between two sheets of baking paper to a thickness of 5 mm (¼ inch). Transfer to a baking tray and chill for 1 hour.

**THE POTATOES**

Cook the potatoes in boiling water for 8 minutes, or until almost tender. Rinse with cold water and pat dry with paper towels. Cut in half.

Put 50 g (1¾ oz) of the butter, the olive oil, bay leaves, garlic, spring onions, lardons and potato halves in a large frying pan. Cook, stirring occasionally, over a low heat, for 3 minutes, or until the butter has melted. Cover with foil to keep warm.

**THE LIVER**

Preheat the oven grill (broiler) to medium–high. Put the remaining butter in a large clean frying pan and place over a medium–high heat until melted. Add the slices of liver and cook for 2 minutes on each side, until browned. Arrange the liver on a baking tray. Cover each slice with the herb crust and place under the grill for 3 minutes, or until the herb crust has softened. Serve immediately, accompanied by the potatoes.

**NOTE**

If you can't get smoked lardons, speck or pancetta work equally well.

# BEEF LIVER WITH BABY ONIONS

**SERVES 6**
**20 MINUTES PREPARATION TIME**
**15 MINUTES COOKING TIME**

4 tomatoes
130 g (4¾ oz) butter
30 baby or pearl onions, peeled
3 garlic cloves
2 tablespoons caster (superfine) sugar
100 ml (3½ fl oz) white port
2 baby cos (romaine) lettuce hearts, leaves separated
Salt and cracked black pepper
6 slices of beef liver (about 750 g/1 lb 10 oz)

**THE VEGETABLES**

Drop the tomatoes into boiling water for 15 seconds, then run them under cold water, remove their skins and cut the flesh into segments.

Melt 50 g (1¾ oz) of the butter in a large frying pan over a low heat. Add the onions, garlic, sugar, white port and a glass of water. Cook over a low heat, shaking the pan from time to time and stirring occasionally. When the liquid has evaporated by a third, add the tomato and lettuce leaves. Season, and cook for 2 minutes, or until the tomatoes have softened slightly.

**THE LIVER**

Cook the remaining butter in another large frying pan over a low heat for 5 minutes, or until the butter is nut brown (noisette). Add the slices of liver and sprinkle over some cracked pepper. Cook over a low heat for 5–10 minutes, constantly spooning over the brown butter, until browned but still a little pink in the centre, or to the desired doneness. Season with salt.

Serve immediately with the vegetables.

# LAMB'S LIVER WITH CARAMELISED APPLES

**SERVES 6**
**15 MINUTES PREPARATION TIME**
**15 MINUTES COOKING TIME**

- 500 ml (17 fl oz/2 cups) freshly pressed apple juice
- Juice of 1 lemon
- 6 granny smith–type apples, peeled and cut into segments
- 110 g (3¾ oz) butter, chilled
- 6 slices of lamb's liver (about 750 g/ 1 lb 10 oz) (see note)
- 2½ tablespoons Calvados (apple brandy)
- Salt and pepper

**THE APPLES**
Put the apple juice in a saucepan and cook over a medium–low heat until reduced by a third.
Put the lemon juice in a bowl and toss the apple segments in the juice.

**COOKING**
Melt 80 g (2¾ oz) of the butter in a large frying pan over a medium heat. Gently brown the apple segments in the butter for 5 minutes on each side. Once golden and caramelised, add the slices of liver and cook for 2 minutes. Pour over the reduced apple juice then add the Calvados and flambé. Let the flame burn out and then stir. Transfer the liver and apples to a serving dish and cover with foil to keep warm.
Add the remaining butter to the pan and whisk until melted and combined with the pan juices. Spoon this over the liver and apples then season and serve.

**NOTE**
Lamb's liver is sometimes called lamb's fry.

# PORK LIVER FRICASSÉE

**SERVES 6**
**30 MINUTES PREPARATION TIME**
**30 MINUTES COOKING TIME**

80 g (2¾ oz) butter, chopped
2 tablespoons sunflower oil
6 waxy potatoes such as charlotte or desiree, peeled and thinly sliced
1 small golden nugget pumpkin (winter squash), seeded, cut into thin wedges and diced into 2 cm (¾ inch) pieces
3 brown onions, thinly sliced
2 carrots, thinly sliced
600 g (1 lb 5 oz) pork liver, deveined and chopped
Salt and pepper
1 bunch of flat-leaf (Italian) parsley, coarsely chopped
4 garlic cloves, coarsely chopped

**THE VEGETABLES**

Heat the butter and sunflower oil in a large frying pan over a low heat until the butter is melted. Add the potato, pumpkin, onion and carrot. Sauté, stirring occasionally, for 15 minutes; they should start to brown.

**THE FRICASSÉE**

Add the liver and cook, stirring occasionally, for another 15 minutes, or until the liver is cooked. Season. Just before serving, sprinkle the fricassée with the chopped parsley and garlic.

# CHICKEN LIVER AND SPINACH SALAD

**SERVES 6**
**10 MINUTES PREPARATION TIME**
**10 MINUTES COOKING TIME**

- 500 g (1 lb 2 oz) chicken livers
- 20 g (¾ oz) butter
- 2 brown onions, thinly sliced
- 2 tablespoons Armagnac brandy
- 200 ml (7 fl oz) veal stock
- Salt and pepper
- 100 ml (3½ fl oz) olive oil
- 1 tablespoon dijon mustard
- 1 tablespoon balsamic vinegar
- 200 g (7 oz) baby spinach

**THE LIVERS**
Check that the chicken livers no longer have their gall bladders (a small green pouch) attached. If they do, remove these with care. Gently melt the butter in a large frying pan over a low heat then sauté the chicken livers and onions in the butter for 5 minutes, or until the livers have browned. Flambé with the Armagnac, then add the veal stock and cook for a further 5 minutes, or until the livers are cooked and the sauce has reduced slightly. Season.

**THE SALAD**
Make a vinaigrette by combining the olive oil, mustard and vinegar in a bowl. Add the spinach and toss to combine. Arrange the salad in shallow bowls, top with the chicken livers and pour over the hot sauce, so the spinach will be partly cooked. Serve immediately.

# STUFFED CABBAGE

**SERVES 6**
**30 MINUTES PREPARATION TIME**
**1 HOUR COOKING TIME**

1 green cabbage (about 1 kg/2 lb 4 oz), leaves separated, thick stem removed
200 g (7 oz) pork scotch fillet, chopped
100 g (3½ oz) pork liver, chopped
150 g (5½ oz) speck (smoked pork belly), sliced into thin matchsticks
4 bulb spring onions (scallions), finely chopped
2 carrots, finely chopped
2 garlic cloves, finely chopped
150 g (5½ oz) cooked, peeled and vacuum-packed chestnuts, crushed (see note)
2 eggs, lightly whisked
Salt and pepper
100 g (3½ oz) caul fat (see note)

**THE CABBAGE**
Cook the cabbage leaves in salted boiling water for 5 minutes, or until tender (in batches if necessary). Drain, rinse under cold water until cool then drain again and pat dry with paper towels.

**THE STUFFING**
Preheat the oven to 180°C (350°F/Gas 4). Pass the fillet and liver through a mincer using a medium–coarse disc. Sauté the speck in a large frying pan over a medium heat without adding any fat, stirring occasionally, until browned and crisp. Next, add the chopped vegetables and garlic and sauté for 5 minutes, or until softened. Incorporate the minced (ground) meat and the chestnuts. Put the mixture into a bowl and cool slightly. Mix in the egg and season generously. Soak the caul fat in warm water to soften then drain carefully and pat dry with paper towels.

**COOKING**
Lay the caul fat out on a clean work surface. Arrange a third of the cabbage leaves on top so they overlap, spoon over a third of the stuffing and repeat until you run out of ingredients. Close up the filling in the caul fat to make a cabbage shape. Bake in a heavy-based casserole dish for 45 minutes, or until golden and cooked.

**NOTE**
The chestnuts can be ordered from specialty gourmet stores. Frozen, blanched chestnuts are also available, but these will need to be cooked in boiling chicken stock for 5 minutes then drained and cooled before using. Caul fat is a thin web-like membrane of fat that covers the stomach of some animals. Most caul fat used in cooking comes from pigs. Order from your butcher ahead of time.

# TERRINE CAMPAGNARDE

**MAKES 1 × 1 KG (2 LB 4 OZ) TERRINE**
**30 MINUTES PREPARATION TIME**
**1 HOUR 45 MINUTES COOKING TIME**
**1 DAY CHILLING TIME**

300 g (10½ oz) pork liver, skin and fat trimmed
300 g (10½ oz) pork jowl
6 pork cheeks, finely diced
150 g (5½ oz) boneless fresh pork belly, rind removed, meat sliced into thin matchsticks
4 brown onions, finely chopped
4 garlic cloves, finely chopped
2½ tablespoons dark rum
150 ml (5 fl oz) thin (pouring) cream
15 g (½ oz) salt
1 teaspoon pepper
12 rashers of streaky bacon
Cornichons and pickled cocktail onions, to serve (optional)

**THE MEATS**
Preheat the oven to 160°C (315°F/Gas 2–3).
Pass the pork liver and pork jowl through a mincer using a medium–coarse disc. Transfer to a large bowl and add the cheek and belly meat.

**THE MIXTURE**
Add the onion, garlic, rum and cream to the meat mixture. Use clean hands to combine. Season.

**THE TERRINE**
Fill a 1.5 litre (52 fl oz/6 cup) capacity terrine dish with the pork mixture, packing it down well to remove any air bubbles, which will oxidise it. Cover the top with the rashers of smoked bacon, overlapping them slightly. Tuck them in so the whole surface of the terrine is well covered. Bake in a bain-marie, uncovered, for 1 hour 45 minutes, or until the internal temperature reaches 70°C (158°F) when tested with a meat thermometer. Once cooked, set on a wire rack and allow to cool in the dish for 1 hour. Place a piece of foil-lined cardboard over the terrine and weigh down with tins of food in the refrigerator for 24 hours before serving.

# PORK TERRINE WITH FRUIT AND NUTS

**MAKES 1 × 1 KG (2 LB 4 OZ) TERRINE**
**30 MINUTES PREPARATION TIME**
**1 HOUR 30 MINUTES COOKING TIME**
**1 DAY CHILLING TIME**

100 g (3½ oz) sultanas (golden raisins)
100 ml (3½ fl oz) Armagnac brandy
350 g (12 oz) pork scotch fillet, chopped
200 g (7 oz) rindless, boneless fresh pork belly, chopped
350 g (12 oz) pork liver, chopped
2 French shallots, finely chopped
180 g (6 oz) pistachios, toasted
180 g (6 oz) skinless hazelnuts, toasted
2 eggs
100 ml (3½ fl oz) white port
15 g (½ oz) salt
1 teaspoon Espelette chilli powder (or substitute with sweet paprika and chilli powder in a 3:1 ratio) (see note)
50 g caul fat (see note on page 20)
100 g (3½ oz) dried apricots
3 tablespoons chestnut or regular honey

**THE PORK AND THE OTHER INGREDIENTS**

Preheat the oven to 160°C (315°F/Gas 2–3).
Place the sultanas and Armagnac in a small saucepan. Just cover with water. Bring to a gentle simmer over a low heat and simmer for 5 minutes then let them stand off the heat to plump up.
Pass all the pork meat through a mincer using a fine mincing disc. Combine this mince with the shallot, 80 g (2¾ oz) of the pistachios, 80 g of the hazelnuts, drained sultanas, eggs, port, salt and chilli powder.
Soak the caul fat in warm water to soften then drain and pat dry with paper towels.

**THE TERRINE**

Fill a 1.25 litre (44 fl oz/5 cup) capacity terrine dish with the pork mixture, packing the mixture down well to avoid air bubbles forming, which can oxidise the terrine. Layer the caul fat evenly over the mixture, tucking in the edges. Bake in a bain-marie, uncovered, for 1½ hours, or until the internal temperature reaches 70°C (158°F) when tested with a meat thermometer. Once cooked, set on a wire rack and allow to cool in the dish for 1 hour. Place a piece of foil-lined cardboard over the terrine and weigh down with tins of food in the refrigerator for 24 hours before serving.

**THE HONEY CONDIMENT**

Coarsely chop the remaining hazelnuts and pistachios in a food processor with the apricots and honey.
Serve this mixture with the terrine.

**NOTE**

Espelette chilli powder is a mild, fruity chilli powder available at specialty food stockists, or online.

# SAGE CRÉPINETTES

**SERVES 6**
**30 MINUTES PREPARATION TIME**
**1 HOUR COOKING TIME**

300 g (10½ oz) pork liver, chopped
300 g (10½ oz) pork scotch fillet, chopped
200 g (7 oz) speck (smoked pork belly)
50 g (1¾ oz) dried black trumpet mushrooms
200 g (7 oz) green cabbage, finely shredded
2 French shallots, finely chopped
2 garlic cloves, finely chopped
Olive oil
12 sage leaves, finely chopped
Salt and pepper
150 g (5½ oz) caul fat (see note on page 20)

**THE MIXTURE**

Preheat the oven to 160°C (315°F/Gas 2–3).
Pass the liver, fillet and speck through a mincer using a medium–coarse mincing disc. Transfer to a bowl. Drop the dried mushrooms in boiling water for 10 minutes, squeeze dry with paper towels and coarsely chop. Soften the cabbage, shallot, garlic and mushroom in a large frying pan over a medium heat with some olive oil. Cool slightly then combine all the ingredients (except the caul fat) and season. Make balls the size of a tennis ball. Soak the caul fat in warm water to soften then drain carefully and pat dry with paper towels. Wrap each meatball in caul fat so it is completely sealed.

**COOKING**

Arrange the meatballs on a baking tray and bake for 1 hour, or until golden brown and cooked through.

**HOW SHOULD I SERVE THEM?**

Hot, with a well-flavoured salad; or cold, with mustard and croutons.

# CHICKEN LIVER SOUFFLÉS

**SERVES 6**
**15 MINUTES PREPARATION TIME**
**35 MINUTES COOKING TIME**

500 g (1 lb 2 oz) chicken livers
2 medium French toast crackers
1 bunch of tarragon, leaves picked
3 garlic cloves
2 tablespoons sunflower oil
60 g (2¼ oz/¼ cup) butter, chopped
50 g (1¾ oz/⅓ cup) plain (all-purpose) flour
500 ml (17 fl oz/2 cups) milk
1 pinch of ground nutmeg
4 eggs, separated
Salt and pepper

**THE LIVER**

Check that the chicken livers no longer have their gall bladders (a small green pouch) attached. If they do, remove these with care. Preheat the oven to 200°C (400°F/Gas 6).

**THE MIXTURE**

Chop the crackers, tarragon leaves and garlic together by hand or in a food processor until very fine.
Heat the sunflower oil in a large frying pan over a high heat. Sauté the chicken livers until brown then transfer to a board and coarsely chop them.
Melt 50 g (1¾ oz) of the butter in a medium saucepan over a medium heat and stir in 40 g (1½ oz) of the flour to make a roux. Gradually, add the milk and nutmeg and cook over a medium heat for 5 minutes, or until the sauce is thick and coats the back of a spoon.
Off the heat, add the liver, crumb mixture and egg yolks. Season.
Beat the egg whites until quite stiff and gently fold half into the mixture until combined. Fold in the remaining egg white until combined.

**COOKING**

Use the remaining butter and flour to grease and flour six 310 ml (10¾ fl oz/1¼ cup) capacity ovenproof ramekins from top to bottom. Fill each one two-thirds full with the mixture, and bake in a bain-marie for 25 minutes, or until puffed and golden. Serve immediately.

**SERVE WITH**

A tomato coulis and creamy mushroom béchamel sauce, for example.

# WARM CHICKEN LIVER MOUSSE

**SERVES 6**
**15 MINUTES PREPARATION TIME**
**15 MINUTES COOKING TIME**

400 g (14 oz) chicken livers
2 tablespoons olive oil
2 French shallots, finely chopped
1 garlic clove, finely chopped
4 juniper berries, crushed
150 ml (5 fl oz) tawny port
150 g (5½ oz) cold lightly salted butter, diced
100 ml (3½ fl oz) thin (pouring) cream
Salt and pepper
Toasted slices of bread, to serve

**THE LIVERS**

Check to make sure the chicken livers no longer have their gall bladders (a small green pouch) attached. If they do, remove these carefully.

**COOKING**

Heat the olive oil in a large frying pan over a medium heat. Brown the livers, shallot, garlic and juniper berries in the oil for a good 5 minutes. Deglaze with the port and cook, stirring, for 4 minutes, or until the liquid reduces to a syrup.

While still warm, transfer everything to the bowl of a food processor and mix with the cold butter until smooth. Add the cream and season to taste. Transfer to a serving bowl and serve with the toasted bread.

**TIP**

Once it has cooled, this mousse becomes a parfait, but be careful, because it oxidises quickly. Cover the surface with plastic wrap or a layer of melted butter. Keep it well chilled in the refrigerator.

# LE GÉSIER
## GIZZARDS

**GIZZARDS:** can be bought fresh or frozen from specialty butchers
if frozen, thaw overnight in the refrigerator before cooking
cut in half to remove the inner pouch and wash carefully

## PART OF A BIRD'S STOMACH THAT PLAYS THE ROLE OF A FOOD MILL

The gizzard is a small pouch full of little stones that has become a concentrated bundle of muscles through its grinding activity. They can make a Schwarzenegger in full possession of his faculties (physical, not intellectual!) green with envy.

The gizzard is a tough customer. Don't think you can appreciate its full tenderness by just pan-frying it, as is, or you will find the results quite surprising, which is to say inedible. The gizzard needs time to soften up. It can't be tamed just like that; it needs pampering to come around. For the gizzard to finally get comfortable and let itself go it needs to have a good soak, with melted duck fat playing the part of the water and bay leaves and thyme playing the role of bath salts. A few hours of bubbles, and there it is, transformed into a tender and tasty morsel to the great delight of a well-seasoned frisée salad.

At that point, the gizzard is ready to play in the big leagues: either pan-fried with a few shallots, deglazed with a good vinegar, or simply grilled… It has found its place at the table, and I love sitting next to it!

# CONFIT GIZZARDS

**SERVES 6**
**45 MINUTES PREPARATION TIME**
**2 HOURS COOKING TIME**

800 g (1 lb 12 oz) fresh duck gizzards
300 g (10½ oz) duck fat
2 sprigs of rosemary
1 tablespoon coarse salt

**THE GIZZARDS**

Open up the gizzards, check that the inner pouch (the hard membrane that grinds up seeds) has been removed. If not, remove and discard. Wash and drain the gizzards. Pat dry with paper towels and remove any silver membrane, leaving just the dark meat.

**COOKING**

Melt the duck fat in a medium saucepan over a low heat then add the gizzards, rosemary and salt. Cook over a low heat for 2 hours. The gizzards are cooked when they are tender. Check for doneness by pricking them with a fork. If it goes in easily, the gizzards are ready.
Place the gizzards in a 1 litre (35 fl oz/4 cup) capacity terrine dish, cover with the cooking fat and store in the refrigerator. They will keep for several months this way as long as they are covered in the duck fat.
The gizzards can be eaten cold, pan-fried, sautéed...
To reheat, simply cook in a little melted duck fat in a frying pan over a medium–low heat for 4–5 minutes or until heated through.

# CASSOULET-STYLE GIZZARDS

**SERVES 6**
**1 NIGHT SOAKING TIME**
**15 MINUTES PREPARATION TIME**
**3 HOURS COOKING TIME**

300 g (10½ oz) dried Tarbais beans (white haricot beans)
4 brown onions, finely chopped
2 carrots, coarsely chopped
6 garlic cloves, finely chopped
3 tablespoons duck fat
3 tablespoons tomato paste (concentrated purée)
Salt and pepper
600 g (1 lb 5 oz) confit gizzards, bought in a jar or tin (see note), or home-made (see page 34)

**THE VEGETABLES**
The night before, cover the beans with cold water and leave to soak. Drain before cooking.

**COOKING**
Gently sauté the chopped vegetables and garlic with the duck fat in a flameproof casserole dish over a medium heat. Add the Tarbais beans then cover with water to at least 5 cm (2 inches) above the beans. Stir in the tomato paste, season and cook, stirring occasionally, over a low heat for 3 hours, or until the beans are tender. Brown the gizzards over a medium–low heat in a frying pan without added fat, stirring occasionally, for 4–5 minutes or until heated through. Drain and serve with the beans.

**NOTE**
Confit duck gizzards in a tin can be purchased from specialty gourmet food stores or ordered online from shops that stock fine French food.

# LES ROGNONS

## KIDNEYS

**BEEF KIDNEYS**
order ahead of time from a specialty butcher
soak in vinegared water for 30 minutes
trim fat if necessary

**VEAL KIDNEYS**
order ahead of time from a specialty butcher
trim fat if necessary
open up to remove the central 'vein'

**LAMB KIDNEYS**
order ahead of time from a specialty butcher
trim fat if necessary
open up to remove the central 'vein'

**PORK KIDNEYS**
order ahead of time from a specialty butcher
soak in vinegared water for 30 minutes
trim fat if necessary

## THE RENAL ORGANS OF CERTAIN ANIMALS AS CONSIDERED FROM A CULINARY POINT OF VIEW

Kidneys come in pairs; they each take a side to filter absolutely everything that passes through the animal. These veritable waste treatment plants, which oddly enough can be delicately made into an economical meal, have become the foil for a whole movement of modern bistronomy.

Fresh kidneys come in a shell of very white fat, which acts as a protective cushion (veal kidneys cooked in their own fat are perfection). This fat can be used in cooking, as when making true *bugnes Lyonnaises*, or simply used as a substitute for a more traditional fat. In these times of crisis, it is a good idea, in any case, to keep your kidneys well covered.

Of all the members of the kidney family, I prefer the veal kidney: its delicate colour, lobed shape, particular texture and subtle flavour put it at the top of its class. It can be prepared in the frying pan and served pink in the middle, or served in a fricassée, lightly deglazed with Cognac and enriched with cream. It belongs in the pantheon of offal. Lamb kidneys have carved out a good niche for themselves. They look like a large dried bean, light brown and firm to the touch. They make friends with the skewer and join the party on the embers of summer. Pork and beef kidneys have a more pronounced taste and a smell that can be somewhat surprising: a bath in vinegared water will make them more welcoming. They are often used in stews or sauces, which cook for long periods of time.

# VEAL KIDNEYS, PURE AND SIMPLE

**SERVES 6**
**15 MINUTES PREPARATION TIME**
**20 MINUTES COOKING TIME**

6 veal kidneys, trimmed of fat by the butcher
100 g (3½ oz) butter, chopped
1 garlic bulb, unpeeled
2 bay leaves
3 French shallots, unpeeled, halved lengthways
1 tablespoon sunflower oil
Fine sea salt and pepper

**THE KIDNEYS**
Using a sharp knife, cut each kidney in half lengthways. Cut out the tough white core ('vein') at the centre, taking care to keep each half intact.

**THE AROMATICS**
Gently melt the butter in a large frying pan over a low heat with the garlic, bay leaves and shallot halves. Cook for 10 minutes, stirring occasionally, spooning the butter over the garlic and shallots at regular intervals.

**COOKING**
Increase the heat to medium–high, add the sunflower oil and brown the kidneys, cut side down, for 5 minutes. Turn them over and cook for 2 more minutes, spooning over the melted butter.
Rest the kidneys in a colander over a bowl for a few minutes so their blood drains away, then season. Serve on a plate with the aromatic butter spooned over.

**TIP**
Be careful, an overcooked kidney will become rubbery. It's best to eat it pink.

# VEAL KIDNEYS IN THEIR FAT

**SERVES 6**
**20 MINUTES PREPARATION TIME**
**10 MINUTES COOKING TIME**

6 whole veal kidneys in their fat
1 tablespoon herbes de Provence (mixed dried herbs)
Fine sea salt and cracked black pepper
150 g (5½ oz) caul fat (see note on page 20)

**THE KIDNEYS**
Preheat the oven to 220°C (425°F/Gas 7).
Carefully remove the kidneys from their fat and remove the thin membrane that covers them. Set the fat aside and discard the membranes. Season the kidneys with the herbs, sea salt and cracked pepper.

**THE FAT**
Using a rolling pin, flatten the fat of each kidney between two sheets of baking paper into a rectangle larger than the size of the kidney. Roll each kidney in its fat.
Soak the caul fat in warm water for 1 minute or until softened slightly. Drain then pat dry with paper towels. Lay on a clean work surface and cut into six even pieces. Wrap each kidney in a piece of caul fat, make a tight package and tie together with kitchen string.

**COOKING**
Place the kidneys in a roasting tin or large casserole dish. Bake, uncovered, for 10 minutes, or until golden and heated through. Remove the string. Serve sliced in the fat.

**SERVE WITH**
A pan of sautéed vegetables with herbs.

# VEAL KIDNEYS AND CEP MUSHROOMS

**SERVES 6**
**30 MINUTES PREPARATION TIME**
**25 MINUTES COOKING TIME**

3 veal kidneys, trimmed of fat by the butcher
800 g (1 lb 12 oz) fresh cep or porcini mushrooms (see note)
1 bunch of curly parsley, leaves picked
150 ml (5 fl oz) thin (pouring) cream
1 bunch of basil, leaves picked
Salt and pepper
50 g (1¾ oz) butter
3 garlic cloves, unpeeled and lightly crushed
1 French shallot, finely chopped

**THE KIDNEYS**
Cut the kidneys into 2 cm (¾ inch) cubes and carefully devein by removing the thick white core.

**THE VEGETABLES AND SAUCE**
Wipe the mushrooms with a clean damp sponge.
Drop the parsley leaves into a saucepan of boiling salted water for 5 seconds. Cool immediately in iced water, then drain. The parsley will then keep all its colour.
Heat the cream in a small saucepan over a low heat then season. Transfer to a food processor with two-thirds of the herbs and process until smooth. Adjust the seasoning.

**COOKING**
Pan-fry the kidneys in a large frying pan with the butter over a high heat. Cook for 5 minutes, or until browned then drain in a colander for 5 minutes.
In the same frying pan, sauté the mushrooms, garlic and shallot over a medium heat for 10 minutes. Return the kidneys to the pan and cook for another 5 minutes, then add the remaining herbs just before serving.
Season lightly and dress with the herb sauce.

**NOTE**
Fresh or frozen cep or porcini mushrooms can be purchased from specialty food suppliers.

# VEAL KIDNEYS IN PORT

**SERVES 6**
**20 MINUTES PREPARATION TIME**
**25 MINUTES COOKING TIME**

3 veal kidneys, trimmed of fat by the butcher
500 g (1 lb 2 oz) parsnips, peeled
50 g (1¾ oz) butter, chopped
2 tablespoons olive oil
4 French shallots, peeled and halved lengthways
200 ml (7 fl oz) tawny port
200 ml (7 fl oz) veal stock
200 g (7 oz) frozen peas
Salt and pepper
1 bunch of chives, snipped

**THE KIDNEYS**
Cut the kidneys into 2 cm (¾ inch) pieces and carefully devein by removing the tough white core in the centre.

**THE VEGETABLES**
Cut the parsnips lengthways into wedges and cook in a saucepan of boiling water for 10 minutes. Drain.

**COOKING**
Meanwhile, melt the butter with the olive oil in a flameproof casserole dish over a medium heat. Brown the kidneys, stirring occasionally, for 5 minutes then drain in a colander for 5 minutes.
Sauté the parsnips and shallots in the same casserole dish over a medium heat for 5 minutes, or until softened. Deglaze with the port then cook for 2–3 minutes, or until reduced by half.
Add the veal stock, kidneys and peas. Cook for another 5 minutes then season and sprinkle with the chives before serving.

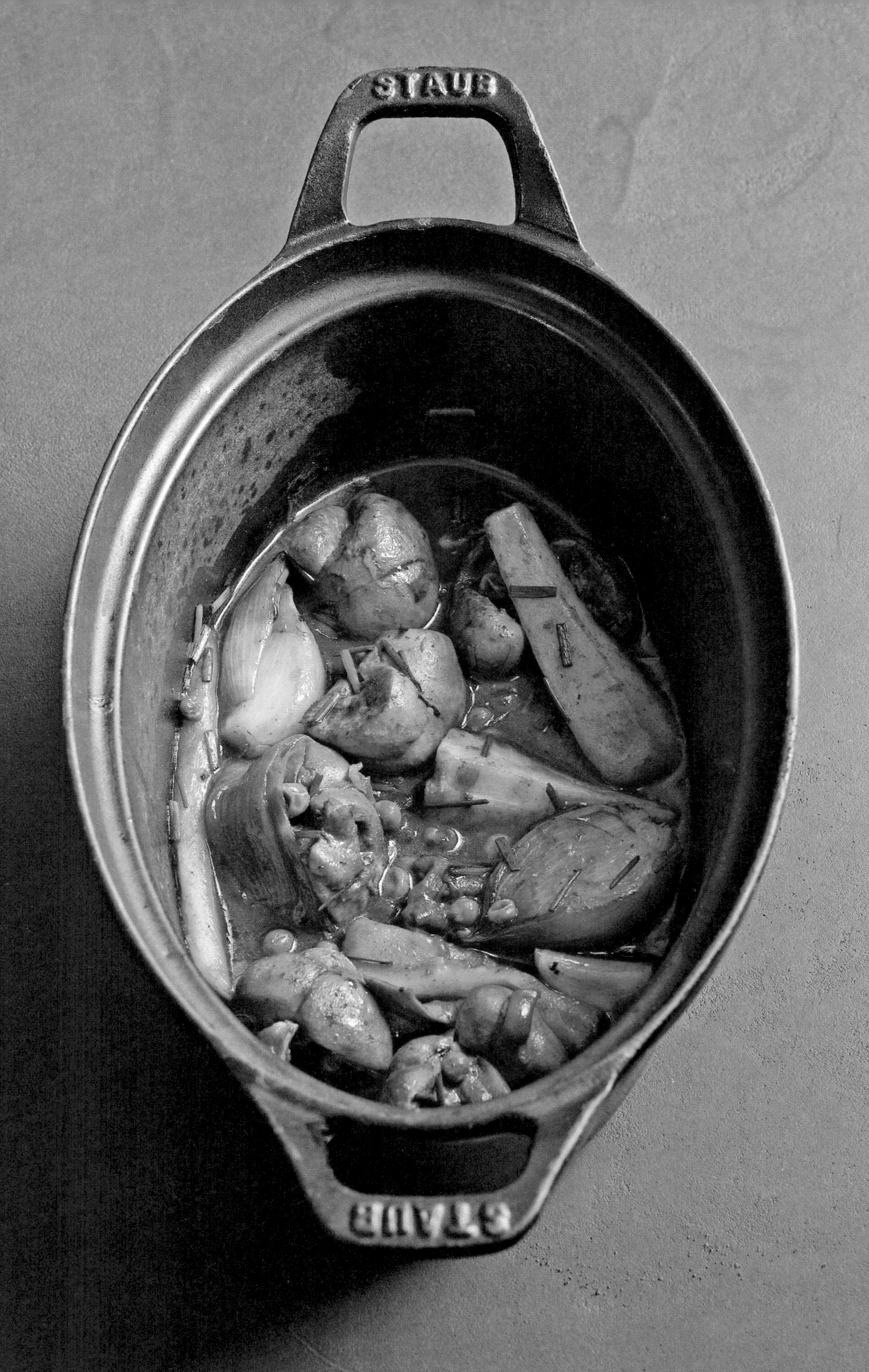
STAUB
STAUB

# BEEF KIDNEYS WITH MUSTARD CREAM

**SERVES 6**
**20 MINUTES PREPARATION TIME**
**30 MINUTES SOAKING TIME**
**45 MINUTES COOKING TIME**

- 3 beef kidneys, trimmed of fat by the butcher
- 60 ml (2 fl oz/¼ cup) white vinegar, for soaking (optional)
- 2 tablespoons olive oil
- 3 onions, coarsely chopped
- 3 carrots, thickly sliced on the diagonal
- 1 fennel bulb, cut into thin wedges
- 1 tablespoon plain (all-purpose) flour
- 200 ml (7 fl oz) dry white wine
- 3 tablespoons wholegrain mustard
- 300 ml (10½ fl oz) thick (double) cream
- 8 sage leaves
- 200 g (7 oz) cooked, peeled and vacuum-packed chestnuts, (see note on page 20)
- Salt and pepper

**THE KIDNEYS**
Cut the kidneys into 2 cm (¾ inch) pieces and carefully devein by removing the tough white core in the centre. If they have a strong smell, soak them for 30 minutes in vinegared water. Drain, rinse well then pat dry with paper towels.
Heat 1 tablespoon of the olive oil in a flameproof casserole dish over a medium high heat. Sauté the kidneys for 5 minutes then drain in a colander for 5 minutes so they lose their blood.

**THE VEGETABLES**
Heat the remaining oil in the same casserole dish over a medium heat. Sauté the onion, carrot and fennel for 5 minutes, or until softened then return the kidneys to the dish. Add the flour, stir, then add the white wine. Bring to a simmer, stirring occasionally, over a low heat for a few minutes then cover and cook, stirring occasionally, for 15 minutes, adding a little water if necessary.

**THE CREAM**
Combine the mustard with the cream then pour into the casserole dish with the kidney mixture. Add the sage and chestnuts then cook, uncovered, for 15 more minutes. Season.

**TIP**
This dish can be prepared a little in advance and gently reheated before serving.

# LAMB KIDNEY KEBABS

**SERVES 6**
**15 MINUTES PREPARATION TIME**
**10 MINUTES COOKING TIME**

- 12 lamb kidneys, trimmed of fat by the butcher
- 12 long sprigs of rosemary, for skewers
- 50 g (1¾ oz) butter
- 1 tablespoon sunflower oil
- 150 ml (5 fl oz) muscat sweet white wine (not fortified)
- 6 garlic cloves, thinly sliced
- 200 ml (7 fl oz) veal stock
- 1 teaspoon tomato paste (concentrated purée)
- 1 bunch of basil, leaves picked
- Salt and pepper

**THE KIDNEYS**
Open the kidneys up widthways, then cut in half and carefully devein by removing the white core.

**THE KEBABS**
Strip the rosemary leaves from the sprigs, leaving just the tops intact. Skewer the kidneys on the sprigs.
In a large frying pan, cook the kebabs in the butter and sunflower oil for 5 minutes over a high heat, turning regularly, until browned. Let them drain on a rack by the oven and cover with foil to keep warm.

**THE SAUCE**
Deglaze the frying pan with the muscat, scraping the bottom of the pan. Add the garlic and reduce the sauce by a third. Add the veal stock, tomato paste and basil then season. Bring to a gentle simmer and reheat the kebabs in this sauce for a few minutes, or until heated through. Serve drizzled with sauce.

**SERVE WITH**
Baked potatoes.

# PORK KIDNEYS WITH PARSLEY BUTTER

**SERVES 6**
**20 MINUTES PREPARATION TIME**
**30 MINUTES SOAKING TIME**
**20 MINUTES COOKING TIME**

12 pork kidneys, trimmed of fat by the butcher
60 ml (2 fl oz/¼ cup) white vinegar, for soaking (optional)
30 g (1 oz) pine nuts
2 garlic cloves, finely chopped
1 French shallot, finely chopped
½ a bunch of curly parsley, coarsely chopped
80 g (2¾ oz) lightly salted butter, softened
6 waxy potatoes such as charlotte or desiree, peeled and sliced into rounds
6 carrots, peeled and sliced into rounds
Salt and pepper

**THE KIDNEYS**
Open up the kidneys and carefully devein by removing the tough white core in the centre. If they have a strong smell, soak them for 30 minutes in vinegared water. Drain, rinse well then pat dry with paper towels.

**THE PARSLEY BUTTER**
Toast the pine nuts in a small dry frying pan over a medium–low heat, tossing frequently, until golden. Coarsely chop then transfer to a bowl and combine with the garlic, shallot, parsley and softened butter using a fork.

**COOKING**
Cook the potatoes and carrots in a saucepan of boiling water for 8–10 minutes, or until just tender. Drain. Melt the parsley butter in a large frying pan over a medium heat then cook the kidneys with the potatoes and carrots, stirring occasionally, for 8–10 minutes or until everything is golden brown. Season and serve.

# VEAL KIDNEY AND SWEETBREADS WITH BLACK TRUMPETS

**SERVES 6**
**30 MINUTES PREPARATION TIME**
**25 MINUTES COOKING TIME**

500 ml (17 fl oz/2 cups) milk
1 tablespoon coarse salt
400 g (14 oz) veal 'heart' sweetbreads
1 veal kidney, trimmed of fat
by the butcher
3 carrots, thickly sliced
40 g (1½ oz) dried black trumpet mushrooms
100 g (3½ oz) butter, chilled and chopped
2 French shallots, thinly sliced
1 tablespoon olive oil
2½ tablespoons Cognac brandy
Salt and pepper

**THE SWEETBREADS AND KIDNEY**
Combine the milk with 1 litre (35 fl oz/4 cups) of water in a large saucepan. Add the coarse salt and the sweetbreads. Bring to the boil then reduce the heat to low and simmer for 15 minutes. Refresh under cold water. Remove the fine membrane from the sweetbreads then devein and cut them into 4 cm (1½ inch) cubes. Cut the kidney into similar size pieces and carefully devein.

**THE VEGETABLES**
Cook the carrots in a saucepan of boiling water for 5 minutes, or until just tender. Drain.
Meanwhile, place the mushrooms in a saucepan and cover with hot water. Bring to the boil over a medium heat and cook for 5 minutes. Remove from the heat and let stand for 5 minutes to rehydrate. Drain, reserving the cooking liquid. Return the cooking liquid to the pan and cook over a medium–high heat until reduced by a quarter.

**COOKING**
Melt half of the butter with the olive oil in a large frying pan over a medium–high heat. Sauté the shallot, then add the mushrooms. Stir in the carrots and sweetbreads and finish with the pieces of kidney. Brown everything then flambé with the Cognac.
Add the reduced mushroom juice, season then use a slotted spoon to transfer the sweetbreads, kidneys and vegetables to a plate. Whisk the remaining cold butter into the cooking juices and serve immediately.

# KIDNEY PIE

**SERVES 6**
**20 MINUTES PREPARATION TIME**
**30 MINUTES CHILLING TIME**
**55 MINUTES COOKING TIME**

3 veal kidneys, trimmed of fat by the butcher
100 g (3½ oz) butter, chopped
50 g (1¾ oz) dried black trumpet mushrooms
6 rashers of bacon, rind removed, chopped
3 bulb spring onions (scallions), finely chopped
2 carrots, cooked and diced
2 parsnips, cooked and diced
1 tablespoon tomato paste (concentrated purée)
200 ml (7 fl oz) veal stock
3 sheets (25 x 25 cm/10 x 10 inches) frozen puff pastry, partially thawed
1 egg yolk, lightly whisked
Salt and pepper

**THE KIDNEYS**
Cut the kidneys into 1.5 cm (⅝ inch) pieces then devein. Melt half of the butter in a frying pan over a medium heat. Brown the kidneys, stirring occasionally, for around 5 minutes. Transfer the kidneys to a colander to drain and leave to rest for 5 minutes.

**THE FILLING**
Place the mushrooms in a heatproof bowl, cover with boiling water and leave to rehydrate for 5 minutes. Drain then squeeze them in a clean tea towel (dish towel) to remove any excess moisture. Melt the remaining butter in a clean frying pan over a medium heat. Sauté the mushrooms, bacon, spring onion, carrot and parsnip. Add the tomato paste and veal stock, then add the kidneys and bring to the boil. Cook, stirring occasionally, for 5 minutes, or until the mixture reaches a syrupy consistency. Season, then transfer to a bowl and cool slightly. Refrigerate until completely cooled.

**THE PIE**
Preheat the oven to 180°C (350°F/Gas 4). Lightly grease a 20 cm (8 inch) spring-form cake tin. Line the base and side of the tin with two pastry sheets, slightly overlapping. Press the pastry sheets together to seal. Trim the pastry, leaving a 1 cm (½ inch) border above the tin. Refrigerate for 30 minutes.
Spoon the cooled filling into the lined tin. Cut a 20 cm (8 inch) circle from the remaining pastry. Moisten the edge then place on top, pressing the pastry edges together to seal. Trim any excess pastry and make a hole in the middle (it will act as a 'chimney'). Glaze the top of the pie with the egg yolk and bake for 45 minutes, or until golden. Stand in the tin for 5 minutes. Serve hot.

# LA TRIPE

## TRIPE

**BEEF TRIPE:** ready to cook (bleached by the butcher)
can be purchased at supermarkets and butchers
may need to be ordered ahead of time

# PART OF THE STOMACH OF AN ANIMAL FOR SLAUGHTER

Tripe is a dish that lines your stomach. Part of the stomach of a cow, tripe is divided into four components. The 'bonnet' or reticulum tripe, honeycomb shaped, helps regurgitate food. It is turned, with mâche lettuce and beetroot, into a *salade de gras-double* (tripe salad) for winter evenings. Don't go through winter without your bonnet! Reed tripe, the abomasum, reminds us again that it's winter. This part, located behind the stomach, helps to digest grass. Its secretions have the property of curdling milk, and so much the better because a meal without cheese is inconceivable. Bible tribe, or the omasum, plays the same role as reed tripe: grinding foods with its multiple leaves. As is always the case with tripe, it takes a very long time to cook. A good book by the fire will help you wait out the time it takes for bible tripe to become tender. Blanket or rumen tripe is the main part of the stomach. Its inner wall is smooth and its outside is lightly honeycombed. The rumen is the reservoir for food; 'Ruminate on what you eat and it will sit well!' Crumbed and bathed in a beurre noisette, it metamorphoses into a top-shelf *tablier de sapeur*.

The tripe trip starts now!

# TRIPE WITH TOMATO AND WHITE WINE

**SERVES 6**
**30 MINUTES PREPARATION TIME**
**6 HOURS COOKING TIME**

- 1.2 kg (2 lb 10 oz) tripe, bleached by the butcher
- 1 calf's foot, boned (see note)
- 200 g (7 oz) pork rind (see note)
- 2 carrots, sliced
- 6 brown onions, finely chopped
- 6 tomatoes, diced
- 5 garlic cloves
- 50 g (1¾ oz) fresh ginger, finely chopped
- 2 tablespoons tomato paste (concentrated purée)
- Bouquet garni
- 2 sprigs of rosemary
- ½ a bunch of flat-leaf (Italian) parsley, chopped
- 1 x 750 ml (26 fl oz) bottle of white wine (Sancerre or sauvignon blanc)
- Salt and pepper

**THE TRIPE**
Preheat the oven to 150°C (300°F/Gas 2).
Cut the tripe into cubes, approximately 4 cm (1½ inches) in size.

**COOKING**
Place the ingredients into a casserole dish. Add enough water so the level of the liquid is 5 cm (2 inches) above the tripe. Season.
Bake, covered, for 6 hours, or until the tripe is tender. Check the amount of liquid at regular intervals; the mixture should always be covered. Add extra water if necessary.

**NOTE**
Calves' feet can be purchased from specialty butchers. Pork rind can be purchased from some supermarkets and most butchers, but may need to be ordered ahead.

# TRIPE WITH CIDER À LA MODE DE CAEN

**SERVES 6**
**30 MINUTES PREPARATION TIME**
**6 HOURS COOKING TIME**

1.2 kg (2 lb 10 oz) tripe, bleached by the butcher
1 calf's foot, boned (see note on page 60)
200 g (7 oz) pork rind (see note on page 60)
6 carrots, sliced
6 brown onions, finely chopped
Bouquet garni
½ a bunch of flat-leaf (Italian) parsley, chopped, plus extra to garnish
4 granny smith–type apples, peeled, cored and cut into wedges
2 × 500 ml (17 fl oz) bottles of dry cider
2½ tablespoons Calvados (apple brandy)
Salt and pepper

**THE TRIPE**
Preheat the oven to 150°C (300°F/Gas 2).
Cut the tripe into cubes, approximately 4 cm (1½ inches) in size.

**COOKING**
Place all the dry ingredients, except for the apples, in a casserole dish. Pour in the cider and Calvados. Add enough water so that the level of the liquid is 5 cm (2 inches) above the tripe. Season.
Bake, covered, for 6 hours. Check the amount of liquid at regular intervals; the mixture should always be covered. Add more water if necessary.
Half an hour before the cooking time is up, add the apples to the casserole. Bake, covered, for a further 30 minutes, or until the apples and tripe are tender.
Remove the pork rind and discard. Season, garnish with the extra parsley and serve.

# TRIPE SALAD

**SERVES 6**
**15 MINUTES PREPARATION TIME**
**4 HOURS COOKING TIME**

600 g (1 lb 5 oz) tripe, bleached by the butcher
4 carrots, peeled
6 brown onions, peeled
1 leek, thickly sliced
1 celery stalk
Bouquet garni
80 ml (2½ fl oz/⅓ cup) sunflower oil
1 tablespoon wholegrain mustard
2 tablespoons white wine vinegar
2 handfuls of fresh and crunchy dandelion leaves (order ahead from selected greengrocers)
Salt and pepper

**THE TRIPE**
Put the tripe in a large saucepan with the carrots, 3 of the onions, the leek, celery and the bouquet garni. Cover with water and cook for 3–4 hours (the tripe should be soft). Drain. Discard the stock and vegetables and slice the tripe into long thin strips.

**COOKING**
Coarsely chop the remaining onions. Add the sunflower oil to a large frying pan over a medium heat. Sweat the onion and allow to soften. Increase the heat to high. Add the strips of tripe and cook, stirring occasionally, for 5 minutes, or until browned.

**THE VINAIGRETTE**
Combine the mustard and vinegar in a bowl then add to the frying pan. Simmer for 2–3 minutes then add the dandelion and toss. Season and serve immediately.

# GRAS-DOUBLE À LA LYONNAISE

**SERVES 6**
**20 MINUTES PREPARATION TIME**
**4 HOURS COOKING TIME**

- 600 g (1 lb 5 oz) tripe, bleached by the butcher
- 4 carrots, peeled
- 3 brown onions, peeled and sliced
- 1 leek, thickly sliced
- 1 celery stalk, coarsely chopped
- Bouquet garni
- 2 tablespoons white wine vinegar
- 2 beetroot (beets), cooked and peeled
- 3 tablespoons dijon mustard
- 120 ml (3¾ fl oz) sunflower oil
- 1 sweet white salad onion, diced
- Juice of 1 lemon
- 200 g (7 oz) mâche lettuce (lamb's lettuce)

**THE TRIPE**
Put the tripe in a large saucepan with the carrots, brown onion, leek, celery and the bouquet garni. Cover with water and cook for 3–4 hours (the tripe should be soft). Drain. Discard the stock and vegetables and slice the tripe into long thin strips. Toss in the vinegar while the tripe is still warm.

**THE SALAD**
Cut the beetroot into large matchsticks. Combine the mustard and oil in a large bowl. Transfer 1 tablespoon of the mustard mixture into a small bowl and set aside for the salad. Toss the tripe with the remaining vinaigrette then add the lemon juice. Serve the tripe lukewarm, adding the beetroot, diced salad onion and mâche lettuce, tossed in the reserved dressing.

# TABLIER DE SAPEUR

**SERVES 6**
**20 MINUTES PREPARATION TIME**
**4 HOURS COOKING TIME**

1 kg (2 lb 4 oz) rumen tripe, bleached by the butcher
4 carrots, peeled
3 brown onions, thickly sliced
1 leek, thickly sliced
1 celery stalk
Bouquet garni
2 eggs
1 tablespoon sunflower oil
6 medium French toast crackers
150 g (5½ oz) butter, chopped
3 bulb spring onions (scallions), thinly sliced
Fine sea salt

**THE TRIPE**
Put the tripe in a large saucepan with the carrots, brown onion, leek, celery and the bouquet garni. Cover with water and cook for 3–4 hours (the tripe should be soft). Drain. Discard the stock and vegetables and slice the tripe into long thin strips. Pat dry with paper towels and cut into six even-sized rectangular pieces.

**CRUMBING**
Whisk the eggs with the sunflower oil in a shallow bowl. Finely chop the crackers in a food processor to a fine crumb. Transfer to a shallow bowl. Dip the tripe in the eggs, then in the breadcrumbs. Arrange these crumbed 'aprons' on a tray lined with baking paper.
Heat the butter in a large frying pan over a medium heat until melted. Add the spring onions and crumbed tripe. Cook the 'aprons' for 3 minutes on each side, or until browned. Sprinkle with sea salt and serve.

**SERVE WITH**
Steamed potatoes and a good béarnaise sauce.

# TRIPOUX

**SERVES 6**
**45 MINUTES PREPARATION TIME**
**6 HOURS COOKING TIME**

6 carrots, peeled
250 g (9 oz) pork belly, finely chopped
100 g (3½ oz) rindless, boneless, cooked ham, finely chopped
100 g (3½ oz) prosciutto, finely chopped
6 garlic cloves, finely chopped
1 bunch of curly parsley, finely chopped
Salt and pepper
1.2 kg (2 lb 10 oz) veal rumen tripe, bleached by the butcher
200 g (7 oz) pork rind (see note on page 60)
1 calf's foot, cut into pieces (see note on page 60)
Bouquet garni
4 brown onions
1 litre (35 fl oz/4 cups) dry white wine
½ a savoy (curly) cabbage, shredded

**THE STUFFING**

Preheat the oven to 150°C (300°F/Gas 2).
Finely chop 2 of the carrots and transfer to a large bowl with the pork belly, ham, prosciutto, garlic and parsley. Season then mix together to create the filling.
Cut the tripe into six even-sized rectangles.
Place a little filling on each rectangle, close up the four sides like a wallet and tie with kitchen string.

**THE STOCK**

Cut the remaining carrots into large sticks and put into a large casserole dish with the tripe parcels, pork rind, calf's foot, bouquet garni and onions. Pour over the white wine and add enough water to cover.

**COOKING**

Bake, covered, for 6 hours, checking the liquid at regular intervals; the mixture should always be covered. Half an hour before the cooking time is up, add the sliced cabbage. Cook for a further 30 minutes, or until the tripe is tender. Season.
Using a slotted spoon, transfer the tripe parcels to a clean board. Remove the string and serve with the carrots, cabbage and cooking juices.

# LE RIS

## SWEETBREADS

**VEAL 'HEART' SWEETBREADS**
can be purchased from specialty butchers
may need to be ordered ahead of time
poach for 15 minutes in water and milk
remove filaments and the outer membrane

**LAMB SWEETBREADS**
can be purchased from specialty butchers
may need to be ordered ahead of time
poach for 15 minutes in water and milk

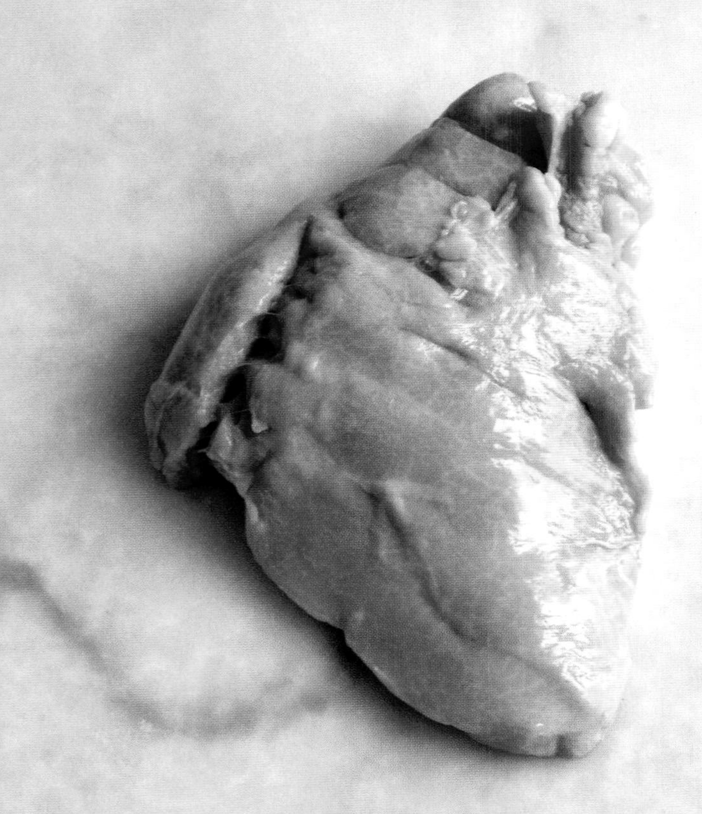

## THE THYMUS GLAND OF CALVES AND LAMBS

Sweetbreads are the perogative of youth. It is a gland located behind the throat of the animal, which disappears with age. 'I'm getting old, it makes me angry as a bull,' a Charolais bull said recently after his sweetbreads disappeared to make way for wrinkles. We note in passing the animal's clumsy use of metaphor, due, I am sure, to an excessive intake of grass.

The gland is composed of two parts: the 'throat' sweetbread, long in shape, fairly fatty, mainly used in fillings, and the 'heart' sweetbread, rounded like an apple — a true gastronomic pleasure, used as a centrepiece. As a gauge of quality, sweetbreads should be as pale as possible; they're a delicate product to be eaten extra-fresh. Sweetbreads need to be soaked for two to three hours in cold water so they lose any trace of blood. The rarity of sweetbreads and the delicacy of their flavour make them an exceptional dish and a true flagship of French cuisine.

# PAN-FRIED SWEETBREADS

**SERVES 6**
**30 MINUTES PREPARATION TIME**
**40 MINUTES COOKING TIME**

500 ml (17 fl oz/2 cups) milk
1 tablespoon coarse salt
900 g (2 lb) veal 'heart' sweetbreads, prepared by the butcher
50 g (1¾ oz) butter, chopped
2 garlic bulbs, top 1 cm (½ inch) removed
3 French shallots, unpeeled, halved lengthways
Salt and pepper

**THE SWEETBREADS**

Combine the milk with 1 litre (35 fl oz/4 cups) of water in a large saucepan. Add the coarse salt and sweetbreads. Bring to the boil then reduce the heat and simmer for 15 minutes. Drain and refresh under cold water. Remove the filaments and any membrane. Gently press the sweetbreads between two sheets of baking paper to flatten, using tinned food or a saucepan of water as a weight. Divide into six even-sized pieces.

**COOKING**

Melt the butter in a frying pan over a low heat. Add the garlic and shallot halves. Cook for 10 minutes, spooning the butter over the garlic and shallots at regular intervals. Increase the heat to medium. Cook for 2 minutes or until the butter turns nut brown (noisette). Reduce the heat to low. Brown the pieces of sweetbread for 5 minutes on each side, spooning over the melted butter during cooking. Season.

**SERVE WITH**

Celery fries, for example.

# SWEETBREADS WITH CREAM

**SERVES 6**
**20 MINUTES PREPARATION TIME**
**35 MINUTES COOKING TIME**

500 ml (17 fl oz/2 cups) milk
1 tablespoon coarse salt
900 g (2 lb) veal 'heart' sweetbreads, prepared by the butcher
50 g (1¾ oz) dried cep (porcini) mushrooms
2 tablespoons olive oil
3 French shallots, thinly sliced
150 ml (5 fl oz) muscat sweet white wine (not fortified)
3 round (or medium long) zucchini (courgettes), halved lengthways and thickly sliced
1 pinch of paprika
300 ml (10½ fl oz) thin (pouring) cream
Salt and pepper

**THE SWEETBREADS**
Combine the milk with 1 litre (35 fl oz/4 cups) of water in a large saucepan. Add the coarse salt and sweetbreads. Bring to the boil then reduce the heat and simmer for 15 minutes. Drain and refresh under cold water. Remove the filaments and membrane. Cut the sweetbreads into cubes, about 4 cm (1½ inches) in size.

**THE MUSHROOM CREAM**
Meanwhile, rehydrate the mushrooms in boiling water for about 5 minutes then drain them.
Heat the olive oil in a flameproof casserole dish over a medium heat. Add the mushrooms and shallot. Cook, stirring occasionally, for 5 minutes, or until softened. Deglaze with the muscat, then add the zucchini, paprika, cream and sweetbreads. Let it reduce for around 10 minutes, then season.

# CRUMBED SWEETBREADS WITH OVERSIZED CHIP

**SERVES 6**
**15 MINUTES PREPARATION TIME**
**45 MINUTES COOKING TIME**

500 ml (17 fl oz/2 cups) milk
1 tablespoon coarse salt
900 g (2 lb) veal 'heart' sweetbreads, prepared by the butcher
35 g (1¼ oz/¼ cup) plain (all-purpose) flour
2 eggs, beaten
150 g (5½ oz/1⅔ cups) flaked almonds
6 waxy potatoes such as charlotte or desiree, peeled
120 g (4¼ oz/1⅓ cups) button mushrooms, thinly sliced
2 garlic cloves, finely chopped
2 tablespoons sunflower oil
200 ml (7 fl oz) veal stock
2 tablespoons liquid coffee and chicory essence
100 g (3½ oz) butter, chilled and chopped
Fine sea salt

**THE SWEETBREADS**
Combine the milk with 1 litre (35 fl oz/4 cups) of water in a large saucepan. Add the coarse salt and sweetbreads. Bring to the boil then reduce the heat and simmer for 15 minutes. Drain and refresh under cold water.
Remove the filaments and membrane. Gently press the sweetbreads between two sheets of baking paper to flatten, using tinned food or a saucepan of water as a weight. Divide into six even-sized pieces.
Place the flour, egg and almonds in separate shallow bowls. Dip the sweetbreads in the flour. Shake off any excess. Dip in the egg and then the almonds, pressing slightly to coat. Transfer to a tray lined with baking paper.

**THE OVERSIZED CHIP**
Trim each potato into a large chip (fry). Cook in a saucepan of boiling water for 15 minutes, or until tender then drain, refresh under cold water and pat dry.

**COOKING**
Sauté the mushrooms and garlic in a frying pan over a medium heat with 1 tablespoon of the sunflower oil until softened. Deglaze with the veal stock, add the coffee and chicory essence then cook for 5 minutes.
Meanwhile, in a non-stick frying pan, brown the potatoes over a low heat with half the butter and the remaining oil until golden and cooked (check with the point of a knife). Transfer to a plate and cover to keep warm. In the same frying pan, brown the sweetbreads on all sides over a low heat.
To serve, whisk the remaining butter into the mushroom sauce. Place a piece of sweetbread, a chip and some sauce on each plate. Season with sea salt.

# LAMB SWEETBREADS WITH VEGETABLES

**SERVES 6**
**30 MINUTES PREPARATION TIME**
**20 MINUTES COOKING TIME**

- 2 carrots, peeled
- 2 waxy potatoes such as charlotte or desiree, unpeeled
- 2 zucchini (courgettes)
- 1 tablespoon coarse salt
- 800 g (1 lb 12 oz) lamb sweetbreads, prepared by the butcher
- 50 g (1¾ oz) butter, chopped
- 1 tablespoon olive oil
- 2 garlic cloves, unpeeled
- 1 brown onion, thinly sliced
- 10 basil leaves, chopped
- Salt and pepper

**THE VEGETABLES**
Cut the carrots into large olive shapes by trimming them gradually with the tip of a knife.
Do the same with the potatoes and zucchini.

**THE SWEETBREADS**
Add the coarse salt and sweetbreads to a saucepan of boiling water. Reduce the heat to low and simmer for 10 minutes. Drain and refresh under cold water then remove any membranes.

**COOKING**
Meanwhile, place the butter, olive oil, garlic and onion in a large frying pan over a medium heat, stirring occasionally until the butter has melted. Cook the potato and carrot in the pan for 10 minutes, or until tender. Add the sweetbreads and cook, turning occasionally, for 3–4 minutes or until browned. Add the zucchini and cook, stirring occasionally, for 5 more minutes or until tender.
When ready to serve, scatter over the chopped basil leaves and season.

# BOUCHÉES À LA REINE

**SERVES 6**
**30 MINUTES PREPARATION TIME**
**30 MINUTES COOKING TIME**

500 ml (17 fl oz/2 cups) milk
1 tablespoon coarse salt
400 g (14 oz) veal 'heart' sweetbreads, prepared by the butcher
200 g (7 oz) frozen puff pastry, thawed
1 egg yolk, lightly beaten
1 tablespoon sunflower oil
150 g (5½ oz) button mushrooms, quartered
3 French shallots, peeled and coarsely chopped
3 chicken quenelles, each sliced into thick rounds (optional)
150 ml (5 fl oz) dry white wine
200 ml (9 fl oz/1 cup) thin (pouring) cream
60 ml (2 fl oz/¼ cup) lobster or prawn bisque
1 pinch of Espelette chilli powder (or substitute with sweet paprika and chilli powder in a 3:1 ratio) (see note on page 24)
Salt and pepper

**THE SWEETBREADS**
Combine the milk with 1 litre (35 fl oz/4 cups) of water in a large saucepan. Add the coarse salt and the sweetbreads. Bring to a boil then reduce the heat to low and simmer for 15 minutes. Drain, refresh under cold water then pat dry with paper towels. Carefully remove the filaments and membrane. Cut the sweetbreads into 5 mm (¼ inch) thick slices.

**THE PUFF**
Preheat the oven to 180°C (350°F/Gas 4). Roll the pastry out on a lightly floured surface. Cut out six 1 cm (¾ inch) thick rounds from the puff pastry. Glaze these with the egg yolk then transfer to a lightly greased baking tray and bake for 20 minutes, or until puffed and golden.

**THE SWEETBREAD CREAM**
Meanwhile, heat the sunflower oil in a large frying pan over a low heat. Add the mushrooms and shallots and cook, stirring occasionally, until softened. Increase the heat to medium then add the sweetbreads and chicken quenelles (if using). Deglaze with the white wine and cook until reduced by a third. Add the cream, bisque and chilli powder. Season then cook for 5 minutes, stirring occasionally, or until the sauce has thickened and coats the back of a spoon.

**THE BOUCHÉES**
Reheat the pastry rounds if necessary, then split them open horizontally. Place a pastry bottom on each serving plate, spoon over some sweetbread cream then top with a pastry lid. Serve immediately so the pastry is still crispy.

# SWEETBREAD PIE

**SERVES 6**
**30 MINUTES PREPARATION TIME**
**1 HOUR 55 MINUTES COOKING TIME**

500 ml (17 fl oz/2 cups) milk
1 tablespoon coarse salt
400 g (14 oz) veal 'heart' sweetbreads, prepared by the butcher
300 g (10½ oz) pork scotch fillet (*échine de cochon*)
60 g (2¼ oz) butter, chopped
150 g (5½ oz) speck (smoked pork belly), cut into thin matchsticks
150 g (5½ oz/1⅔ cups) button mushrooms, thinly sliced
4 French shallots, finely chopped
100 ml (3½ fl oz) white port
150 ml (5 fl oz) thin (pouring) cream
Salt and pepper
Plain (all-purpose) flour, for dusting
2 sheets (25 x 25 cm/10 x 10 inches) frozen puff pastry, partially thawed
1 egg yolk, lightly whisked

**THE SWEETBREADS**
Combine the milk with 1 litre (35 fl oz/4 cups) of water in a large saucepan. Add the coarse salt and sweetbreads. Bring to the boil then reduce the heat and simmer for 15 minutes. Drain and refresh under cold water. Remove the filaments and membrane. Cut the sweetbreads into 1 cm (½ inch) cubes.

**THE FILLING**
Mince the pork fillet in a mincer using a medium–coarse mincing disc. Transfer to a bowl.
Melt 50 g (1¾ oz) of the butter in a large frying pan over a medium heat. Sauté the sweetbreads, speck, mushroom and shallot, stirring occasionally, for 10 minutes, or until the vegetables have softened. Add the port and cream and reduce until all the liquid has been absorbed. Cool slightly then add to the minced (ground) pork. Mix well, season then cool.

**THE PIE**
Preheat the oven to 160°C (315°F/Gas 2–3).
Butter and flour a 10 x 20 cm (4 x 8 inch) loaf (bar) tin or terrine dish. Line the base and sides of the tin with a sheet of pastry, trimming to fit. Allow the pastry to overhang by 1 cm (½ inch). Add the filling. Cut the remaining pastry to fit the top of the pie. Moisten the edges then place on top and join with the other sheet of pastry. Glaze with the egg yolk and make a hole in the middle (it will act as a 'chimney'). Bake for 1½ hours, or until golden. Stand in the tin for 5 minutes. Serve lukewarm or cold.

# LE CŒUR

## HEART

**BEEF, VEAL, LAMB OR DUCK HEART**
can be purchased fresh or frozen from specialty butchers or poultry stores
may need to be ordered ahead of time
if frozen, thaw in fridge overnight
remove the veins at the base

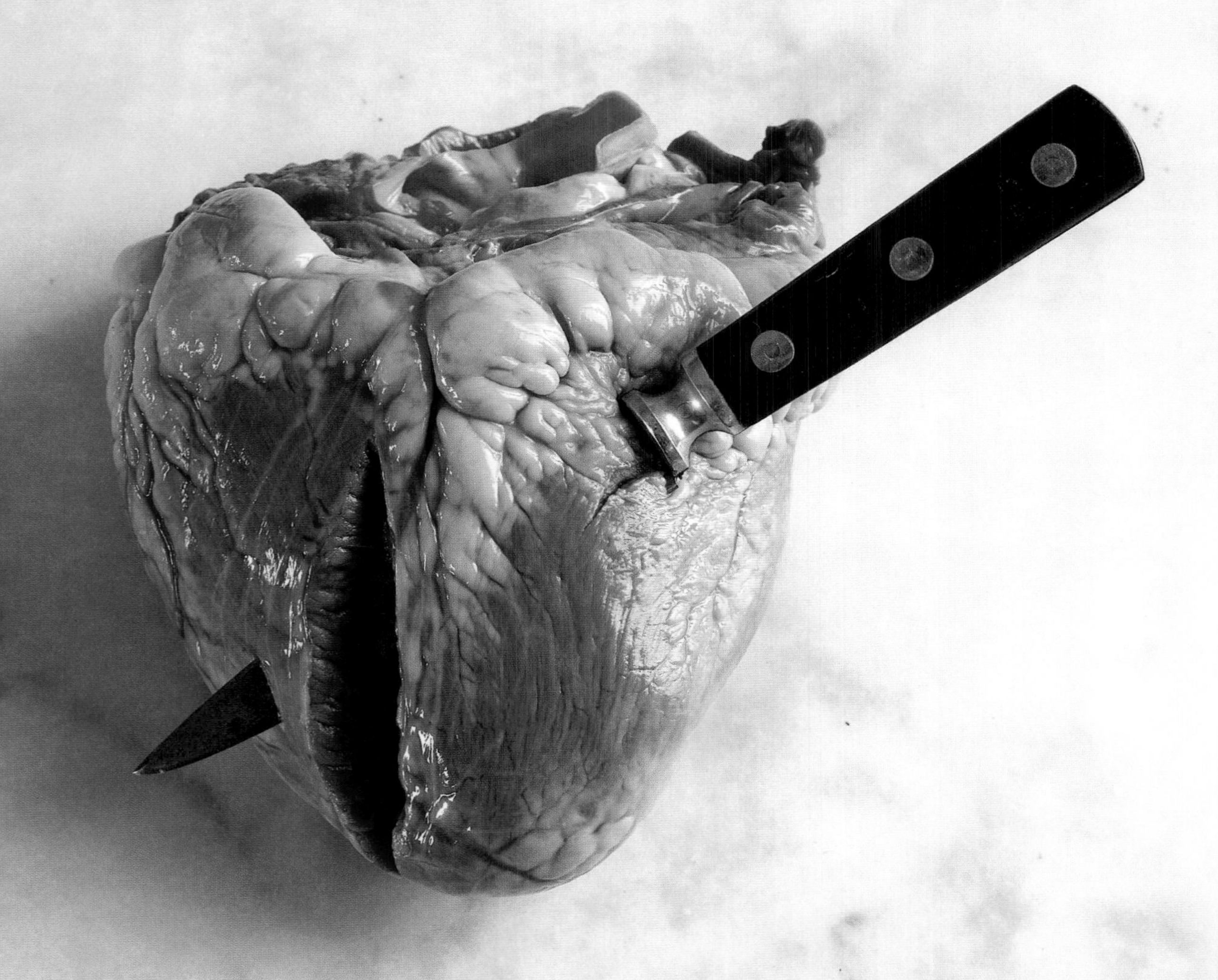

## A HOLLOW, MUSCULAR ORGAN, OVOID IN SHAPE AND LOCATED IN THE THORACIC CAVITY. THE CENTRAL MOTOR FOR CIRCULATING BLOOD

Given such a definition, sensitive souls and delicate taste buds quiver in anticipation at the idea of sampling this delicacy. High in protein: 'Have some heart, you'll be strong!' Low in fat: 'Small belly, big heart!' It's high time we brought the benefits of this choice food, full of emotion, up to date. The heart has a simple and democratic generosity that's all its own: 'If you have many riches, give some of your wealth; if you have little, give your heart.' In fact, you need heart to cook. 'Ah! You have such a good heart!' another friend told me, tears in his eyes, remembering a fine, generous and tasty dish.

We offer our hearts to give pleasure (the duck is a perfect example) and we open our hearts to share pleasure, as a well-bred calf would say. Don't overdo it, though — heartburn can quickly spoil the moment.

# PAN-FRIED DUCK HEARTS WITH GINGER

**SERVES 4**
**20 MINUTES PREPARATION TIME**
**15 MINUTES COOKING TIME**

400 g (14 oz) duck hearts
50 g (1¾ oz) butter, chopped
150 g (5½ oz) speck (smoked pork belly), rind removed, cut into lardons
12 garlic cloves, unpeeled
20 g (¾ oz) fresh ginger, cut into thin matchsticks
200 g (7 oz) water chestnuts (see note)
1 bunch of chives, snipped
Salt and pepper

**THE HEARTS**
Prepare the duck hearts by removing the veins at the base.

**COOKING**
Melt the butter in a large non-stick frying pan over a medium–high heat. Brown the speck with the garlic and ginger for around 5 minutes, stirring occasionally. Add the duck hearts and water chestnuts and cook, stirring occasionally, for a good 5 minutes, or until the duck hearts have browned. Add the chives and season.

**HOW SHOULD I SERVE THEM?**
As a chic nibble with drinks to wow your guests.

**NOTE**
Cooked frozen water chestnuts that have been thawed or tinned water chestnuts that have been drained can both be used for this dish.

# BEEF HEART ST JOSEPH

**SERVES 6**
**20 MINUTES PREPARATION TIME**
**2 HOURS 25 MINUTES COOKING TIME**

1 beef heart
50 g (1¾ oz) butter, chopped
6 French shallots, sliced
1 tablespoon plain (all-purpose) flour
1 x 750 ml (26 fl oz) bottle of red wine
  (a shiraz or Côtes du Rhône works well)
200 ml (7 fl oz) veal stock
100 ml (3½ fl oz) crème de cassis
  (blackcurrant liqueur)
500 g (1 lb 2 oz) frozen blueberries
2 sticks of liquorice root
3 star anise
Salt and pepper

**THE HEART**
Slice the beef heart thinly and devein.

**COOKING**
Melt the butter in a flameproof casserole dish over a medium heat. Sauté the heart and shallot until the heart has browned. Stir in the flour until combined. Add the wine then gently reduce by half.
Add the stock, crème de cassis, blueberries, liquorice root and star anise. Bring to the boil. Cover and cook over a low heat, stirring occasionally, for 2 hours: the heart should be very tender. Season.

**SERVE WITH**
A good parsnip purée, for example.

STAUB

# VEAL HEARTS WITH CREAM, ORANGE AND SAFFRON

**SERVES 6**
**45 MINUTES PREPARATION TIME**
**1 HOUR 5 MINUTES COOKING TIME**

2 veal hearts
1 orange
4 cloves
500 g (1 lb 2 oz) frozen or fresh broad beans
50 g (1¾ oz) butter
12 baby onions, peeled
1 tablespoon plain (all-purpose) flour
300 ml (10½ fl oz) sweet white wine
(Monbazillac works well)
1 teaspoon curry powder
1 pinch of saffron threads
300 ml (10½ fl oz) thin (pouring) cream
Salt and pepper

**THE HEARTS**
Slice the veal hearts thinly and devein.

**THE REST**
Finely grate the zest from half the orange and squeeze its juice. Stud the other orange half with the cloves. Drop the beans in boiling salted water for 20 seconds. Drain. Refresh immediately with cold water then peel.

**COOKING**
Melt the butter in a large deep frying pan over a medium heat. Sauté the onions with the sliced hearts, until browned, then stir in the flour. Add the wine, orange juice and zest, the orange half studded with cloves, the curry powder and saffron. Bring to the boil then cook over a low heat, stirring occasionally, for 45 minutes. Stir in the cream and continue cooking for 15 minutes, or until the heart meat is tender. Season and add the broad beans just before serving.

# LAMB HEARTS WITH CORIANDER AND PINE NUTS

**SERVES 6**
**30 MINUTES PREPARATION TIME**
**15 MINUTES COOKING TIME**

6 lamb hearts
Vegetable oil, for deep-frying
1 handful of coriander (cilantro) sprigs
60 g (2¼ oz/¼ cup) butter, chopped
2 brown onions, thinly sliced
50 g (1¾ oz) fresh ginger, peeled and cut into thin matchsticks
Zest and juice of 1 lemon
60 g (2¼ oz) pine nuts
Salt and pepper

**THE HEARTS**
Halve and devein the lamb hearts.

**COOKING**
Heat some vegetable oil in a frying pan over a medium–high heat and fry the coriander sprigs until crisp. Drain on paper towels.
Melt 40 g (1½ oz) of the butter in a large frying pan over a medium heat then add the hearts and sauté with the onion, ginger, lemon zest and pine nuts. Cook, stirring occasionally, for 10 minutes or until browned. Season. Remove the hearts to a serving dish and cover with foil to keep warm.
Add the lemon juice to the pan to deglaze. Whisk in the remaining butter then pour this pan sauce over the hearts and garnish with sprigs of fried coriander.

**SERVE WITH**
A home-made piperade.

# LE PIED

## FEET

**CALF, LAMB OR PIG FEET**
can be purchased from specialty butchers
may need to be ordered ahead of time
ready to cook
if frozen, thaw in refrigerator overnight

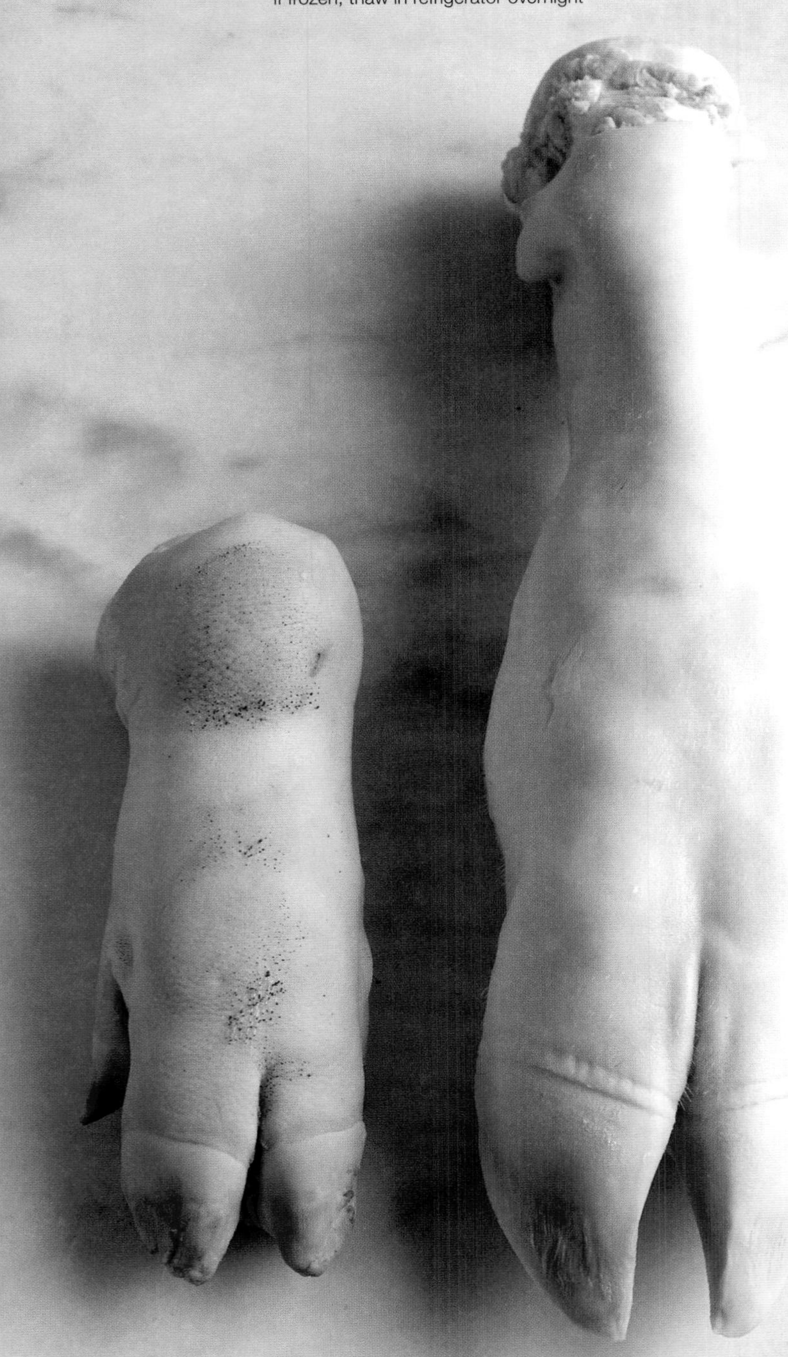

# PART OF THE EXTREMITY OF THE LEG, BEARING WEIGHT AND ALLOWING LOCOMOTION

The foot is probably the richest offal meat. With elevated levels of fat and cholesterol, it comes across as a high-calorie food. However, its long cooking time (the time it takes to turn it into a soft and tasty delicacy) naturally renders out its fat and makes it more accessible in nutritional terms. It is essentially made of collagen, a particularly dense tissue used in dishes like aspic or *boeuf à la mode* to give the sauce a gelatinous consistency.

The foot is usually sold blanched and ready to cook. Pig trotters can be enjoyed grilled with a good vinaigrette, boned in a crépinette, or crumbed and then baked. Calf's foot is prepared as a salad with onions, it fills the afternoon with its fragrance. It has, in short, conquered the wooden table and chequered tablecloth to the great joy of bistro aficionados.

If, by chance, the lovely creature sitting opposite you suggests with a naughty smile that you play footsies, rise to the occasion, forget about food and go for it.

# GRILLED PIG TROTTERS

**SERVES 6**
**20 MINUTES PREPARATION TIME**
**3 HOURS 30 MINUTES COOKING TIME**

6 pig feet (trotters), prepared by the butcher
4 carrots, peeled and coarsely chopped
3 brown onions, peeled and coarsely chopped
1 leek, coarsely chopped
1 celery stalk, coarsely chopped
1 tablespoon coarse salt
Bouquet garni
2 tablespoons wholegrain mustard
2 tablespoons sherry vinegar
2 tablespoons Maggi seasoning sauce
90 ml (3 fl oz) olive oil
1 bunch of tarragon, leaves picked
1 French shallot, finely chopped
Salt and pepper

**THE TROTTERS**
Place the trotters in a large saucepan of water with the carrot, onion, leek, celery, coarse salt and the bouquet garni. Bring to a simmer over a medium heat. Reduce the heat to low and cook for 3 hours, or until the trotters are tender.
Remove the trotters using a slotted spoon and drain. Preheat the oven grill (broiler) to a medium–high heat. Line a baking tray with greased foil. Arrange the trotters on the tray and place under the grill for 10 minutes on each side, or until golden.

**THE VINAIGRETTE**
Combine the mustard, vinegar, seasoning sauce, olive oil, tarragon and shallot in a bowl. Season. Serve the trotters dressed with the vinaigrette.

# PIG TROTTERS EN CRÉPINETTE

**SERVES 6**
**45 MINUTES PREPARATION TIME**
**30 MINUTES CHILLING TIME**
**3 HOURS 30 MINUTES COOKING TIME**

- 6 pig feet (trotters), prepared by the butcher
- 4 carrots, peeled and cut into thirds
- 3 brown onions, peeled and coarsely chopped
- 1 leek, cut into thirds
- 1 celery stalk, cut into thirds
- 1 tablespoon coarse salt
- Bouquet garni
- 2 tablespoons olive oil
- 3 bulb spring onions (scallions), finely chopped
- 3 leaves of silverbeet (Swiss chard), green parts only, shredded
- 200 g (7 oz) foie gras, coarsely chopped (see note)
- 1 teaspoon Espelette chilli powder (or substitute with sweet paprika and chilli powder in a 3:1 ratio) (see note on page 24)
- 3 medium French toast crackers, finely crushed
- Salt and pepper
- 50 g (1¾ oz) caul fat (see note on page 20)

### THE TROTTERS

Put the trotters in a large saucepan of water with the carrot, brown onion, leek, celery, coarse salt and the bouquet garni. Bring to a simmer over a medium heat. Reduce the heat to low and simmer for 3 hours, or until the trotters are very tender and the meat is falling off the bone. Remove the trotters and vegetables and cool until lukewarm. Bone the trotters then finely dice the meat, skin and vegetables.

### THE CRÉPINETTES

Heat the olive oil in a large frying pan over a medium heat. Add the diced ingredients to the pan with the spring onions, silverbeet, foie gras and Espelette powder. Cook, stirring occasionally, for 10 minutes, or until softened. Stir in the crushed crackers until well mixed and then season.

Soak the caul fat in warm water for 1 minute, or until softened. Drain, rinse then pat dry with paper towels. Carefully lay the caul fat out on a clean work surface. Roll the trotter mixture into golf ball–sized portions and wrap each one in caul fat. Arrange the crépinettes on a baking tray and chill for 30 minutes.

Preheat the oven to 200°C (400°F/Gas 6) and bake the crépinettes for 8–10 minutes, or until golden.

### HOW SHOULD I SERVE THEM?

As an aperitif, with mustard or a spicy condiment.

### NOTE

If fresh foie gras isn't available, look for semi-cooked and cooked foie gras, which is available vacuum-packed in tins or jars from French food grocers or specialty food stores. Alternatively, use semi-cooked chicken livers.

# PIG TROTTER AND DANDELION SALAD

**SERVES 6**
**45 MINUTES PREPARATION TIME**
**30 MINUTES CHILLING TIME**
**3 HOURS 30 MINUTES COOKING TIME**

6 pig feet (trotters), prepared by the butcher
4 carrots, coarsely chopped
3 brown onions, coarsely chopped
1 leek (white part only), coarsely chopped
1 celery stalk, coarsely chopped
1 tablespoon coarse salt
Bouquet garni
50 g (1¾ oz/⅓ cup) skinless hazelnuts, toasted and coarsely crushed
50 g (1¾ oz) pistachios, toasted and coarsely crushed
1 French shallot, finely chopped
20 g (¾ oz) fresh ginger, finely grated
Salt and pepper
90 ml (3 fl oz) walnut oil
250 g (9 oz) fresh and crunchy dandelion leaves (order ahead from selected greengrocers)
2 tablespoons balsamic vinegar

**THE TROTTERS**
Put the trotters in a large saucepan of water with the carrot, onion, leek, celery, coarse salt and the bouquet garni. Bring to a simmer over a medium heat. Reduce the heat to low and simmer for 3 hours, or until the trotters are very tender and the meat is falling off the bone. Remove the trotters and vegetables and cool until lukewarm. Bone the trotters while still warm. Finely dice the meat, skin and vegetables and mix together.

**THE SAUSAGES**
Mix the hazelnuts, pistachios, shallot and ginger into the trotter mixture and season. Form into large sausages — how many will depend on the size of the slices you want at the end — and roll each tightly in plastic wrap, twisting the ends. Chill for 30 minutes, or until firm.

**COOKING**
Cut the sausages into 1 cm (½ inch) thick slices. Heat some walnut oil in a large non-stick frying pan over a medium–high heat. Cook the sausage slices in batches for 2 minutes on each side, or until browned. Serve immediately with the dandelion leaves dressed with balsamic vinegar and remaining walnut oil.

# CALF'S FOOT SALAD

**SERVES 6**
**30 MINUTES PREPARATION TIME**
**2 HOURS 30 MINUTES COOKING TIME**

3 calf feet, prepared by the butcher
Bouquet garni
12 Jerusalem artichokes, peeled
125 ml (4 fl oz/½ cup) olive oil
50 g (1¾ oz/⅓ cup) pine nuts
1 egg, hard-boiled
1 tablespoon dijon mustard
2 tablespoons white wine vinegar
100 ml (3½ fl oz) neutral oil
  (such as sunflower or canola)
Salt and pepper
1 bunch of coriander (cilantro),
  leaves picked
1 French shallot, thinly sliced

**THE FEET**
Put the calf feet and bouquet garni in a large stockpot. Cover with water, bring to the boil and skim until no more scum rises to the surface. Leave to boil for 2 hours, or until the feet are very tender and the meat is falling off the bone. Transfer the feet to a bowl and cool slightly.
Bone them when lukewarm, removing all the small bones by hand. The meat should come off easily. Discard the bones. Finely dice the meat.

**THE JERUSALEM ARTICHOKES**
Cook the artichokes in a saucepan of boiling water for 10 minutes, or until tender. Drain, then cut into wedges. Heat 1 tablespoon of the olive oil in a frying pan over a medium heat. Brown the artichokes on all sides and add the pine nuts.

**THE MAYONNAISE**
Mash the egg with a whisk in a bowl. Add the mustard, vinegar and remaining olive oil and the sunflower or canola oil. Whisk until combined then season.
Combine the diced meat with the mayonnaise, coriander and shallot. Serve with the warm Jerusalem artichokes and pine nuts.

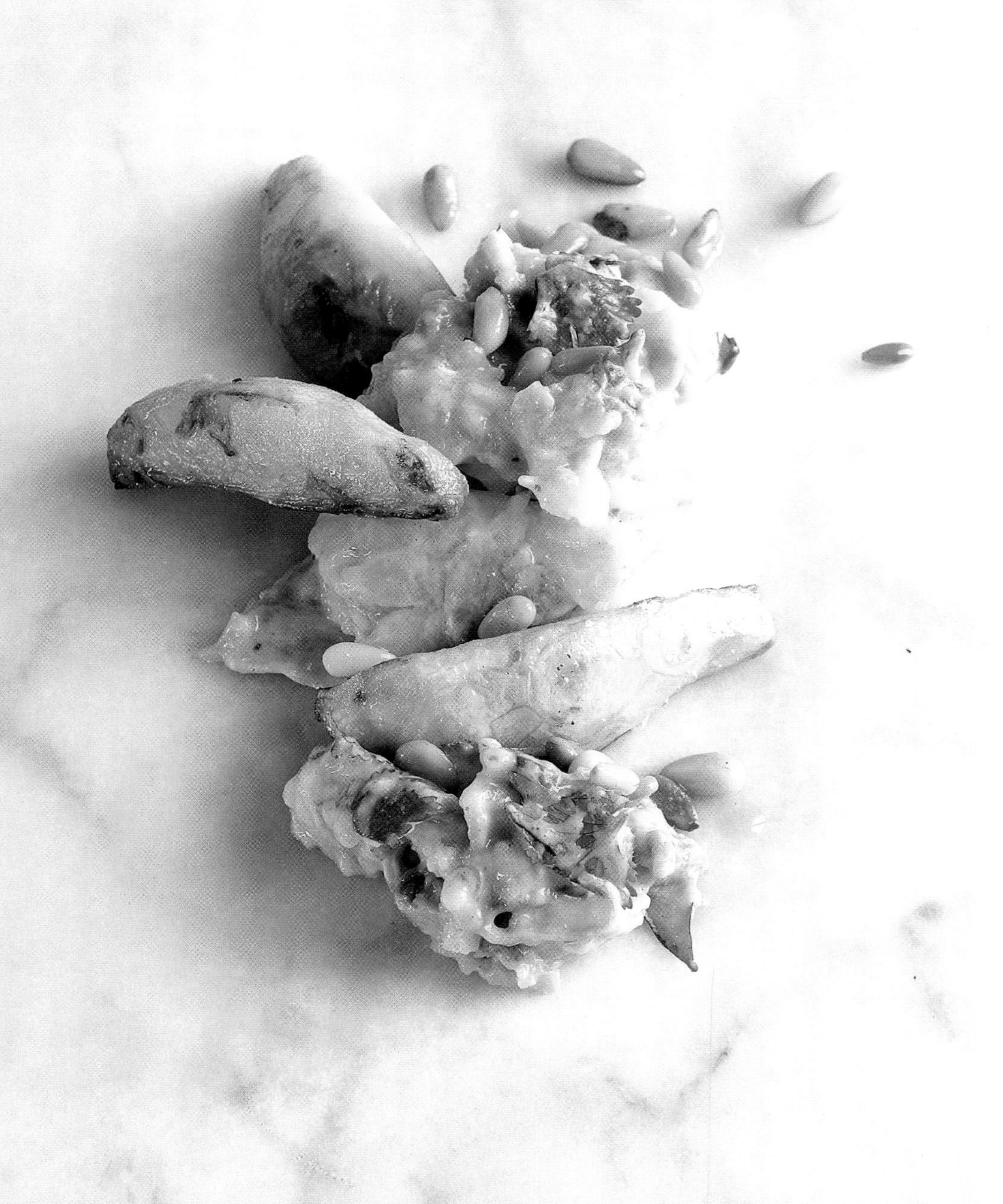

# PIEDS PAQUETS

**SERVES 6**
**20 MINUTES PREPARATION TIME**
**5 HOURS 10 MINUTES COOKING TIME**

- Stuffing for the tripe parcels (page 70)
- 1.2 kg (2 lb 10 oz) lamb tripe, prepared by the butcher, cut into 18 even-sized pieces (see note)
- 200 g (7 oz) speck (smoked pork belly), rind removed, cut into lardons
- 6 garlic cloves, coarsely chopped
- 4 brown onions, coarsely chopped
- 12 sheep's feet, prepared by the butcher (see note)
- 6 tomatoes, cut into wedges
- 2 red capsicums (peppers), sliced into strips
- Bouquet garni
- 2 litres (70 fl oz/8 cups) dry white wine
- 1 bunch of flat-leaf (Italian) parsley, coarsely chopped
- 6 carrots, peeled and cut into thick batons
- 6 parsnips, peeled and cut into thick batons
- Salt and pepper

**THE STUFFING**
Preheat the oven to 150°C (300°F/Gas 2). Make the stuffing on page 70 then wrap that in the pieces of lamb tripe to make 18 small 'packets'. Put aside. Gently sauté the speck, garlic and onion together in a large flameproof casserole dish over a medium heat. Cook, stirring occasionally, for 10 minutes, or until softened.

**COOKING**
Add the feet, stuffed tripe packets, tomato, capsicum and the bouquet garni to the dish. Pour over the white wine and enough water to cover by at least 5 cm (2 inches). Cover and bake in the oven for 4 hours. Add the parsley to the casserole with the carrot and parsnip. Cook for a further 1 hour, or until the feet and tripe packets are tender. Season. Remove and discard the string from the tripe packets then return to the casserole dish. Serve.

**NOTE**
Lamb tripe and sheep's feet can be purchased from specialty butchers but may need to be ordered ahead of time.

# LA QUEUE

## TAIL

**OXTAIL:** available from select butchers
may need to be ordered ahead of time
scald to remove impurities

**PIG'S TAIL:** ready to cook

## BODY PART OF MANY VERTEBRATES, POSTERIOR TO THE ANUS, OFTEN ELONGATED AND FLEXIBLE

The tail — *la queue* — is synonymous with winter. It brings slow-cooking to the fore; the cooking that takes its time to draw out the best; the cooking that gives us red cheeks. It's the time of long simmerings, when the kitchen windows fog up with leek steam so you can draw patterns on the glass panes. You stay at home listening to the burbling 'ploplop' of the stove, life is good.

Oxtail is a master of delayed gratification. It is covered in a tasty, fibrous meat meant for long and gentle cooking in a pot full of flavours; patience is the order of the day. The meat, to be at its best, should completely fall off the bone — the tail is finally stripped bare.

Oxtail pot-au-feu with boiled vegetables, 'parmentiers' with mashed potatoes, and 'royals' in a sauce… it is alive and well and always active. Pig's tail has more fat and its cooking time is shorter. It joyfully takes to cooking in broth to become as soft as a pillow on a tired night; it sleeps peacefully in the oven to become as bronzed as a tanning addict at the height of summer; it is also full of vigour.

Such is its nobility that the most fervent defenders of its gastronomic qualities, the head chefs of the aristocracy, are given the title of *maître queux* (a rather X-rated title in French-speaking lands). Doff your hats!

# OXTAIL PARMENTIER

**SERVES 6**
**45 MINUTES PREPARATION TIME**
**4 HOURS COOKING TIME**

2 oxtails, cut into pieces by the butcher
2 brown onions, peeled
4 cloves
1 leek, cut into large chunks
4 carrots, peeled and cut into large chunks
1 celeriac, peeled and cut into large chunks
Bouquet garni
1 tablespoon coarse salt
6 large baking potatoes, peeled
2 French shallots, finely chopped
Salt and pepper
180 g (6 oz) lightly salted butter

**CRUMBLE**

50 g (1¾ oz) unsalted butter
50 g (1¾ oz/⅓ cup) plain (all-purpose) flour
50 g (1¾ oz/½ cup) walnuts, coarsely chopped
30 g (1 oz) brown sugar

**THE TAILS**

Blanching the oxtails removes any impurities. To blanch, place the oxtail pieces in a large saucepan of water. Bring to the boil. Drain, then rinse.

**COOKING**

Stud the onions with the cloves. Place the oxtail pieces in a saucepan of fresh boiling water, this time adding the leek, carrot, celeriac, clove-studded onions and the bouquet garni. Gently simmer for 3 hours, or until the meat is falling off the bone. Remove the meat and vegetables from the cooking liquid with a slotted spoon. Add the coarse salt and potatoes to the cooking liquid. Bring to a simmer and cook for 30 minutes. Drain, reserving 250 ml (9 fl oz/1 cup) of the liquid.
Meanwhile, debone the tails. Shred the meat and place in a bowl. Dice the carrots, leek and celeriac into 1 cm (½ inch) pieces. Add to the oxtail meat with the shallot then mix together and season.

**THE MASH AND CRUMBLE**

Preheat the oven to 180°C (350°F/Gas 4).
Mash the potatoes with the butter and enough of the cooking liquid to form a smooth mash. Season.
Microwave the butter for the crumble in a microwave-safe bowl on high for 30 seconds, or until melted. Add the flour, walnuts and sugar and mix well.
Place the oxtail mixture in an ovenproof dish, top with the mashed potatoes and sprinkle with the crumble. Bake for 15 minutes, finishing under the grill for 5 minutes to brown the top.

# OXTAIL À LA ROYALE

**SERVES 6**
**30 MINUTES PREPARATION TIME**
**4 HOURS COOKING TIME**

2 oxtails, cut into pieces by the butcher
2 brown onions, peeled
4 cloves
2 tablespoons olive oil
200 g (7 oz) speck (smoked pork belly), rind removed, cut into thin matchsticks
4 carrots, peeled and sliced
1 leek, white part only, peeled
6 French shallots, thinly sliced
6 garlic cloves, thinly sliced
2 tablespoons plain (all-purpose) flour
2 litres (70 fl oz/8 cups) red wine (Côtes du Rhône style works well)
Bouquet garni
1 tablespoon coarse salt
1 orange
100 g (3½ oz) foie gras, diced (see note)
Salt and pepper
1 bunch of tarragon, leaves picked

**THE TAILS**
Blanching the oxtails removes any impurities. To blanch, place the oxtail pieces in a large saucepan of water. Bring to the boil. Drain, then rinse.

**COOKING**
Stud the onions with the cloves.
Heat the olive oil in a large flameproof casserole dish over a medium heat. Cook the oxtail, in batches, for 5 minutes on each side, or until browned. Transfer to a plate. Add the speck to the casserole dish. Cook, stirring occasionally, for 3 minutes or until browned. Return the oxtail to the dish. Add the carrot, onions, leek, shallot and garlic. Stir in the flour. Add the wine, bouquet garni and coarse salt. Simmer, uncovered, for 3 hours, or until the meat is falling off the bone.
Debone the oxtail. Shred the meat and place into a bowl. Cover to keep warm.
Remove the bouquet garni from the cooking liquid. Coarsely grate the zest of the orange. Mix the cooking liquid and vegetables, in batches, in a food processor until smooth. Add the foie gras, squeeze in the juice of the orange and process again. Return the mixture to the casserole dish. Season. Stir in the meat. Garnish with tarragon leaves and orange zest.

**SERVE WITH**
Orange wedges and a good chestnut purée.

**NOTE**
If fresh foie gras is not available, look for semi-cooked and cooked foie gras, which is availalbe vacuum-packed in tins or jars from French food grocers or specialty gourmet food stores. If it's not available, substitute with 75 g (2¾ oz) of chopped butter.

# OXTAIL POT-AU-FEU

**SERVES 6**
**20 MINUTES PREPARATION TIME**
**4 HOURS COOKING TIME**

1 oxtail, cut into six pieces by the butcher
2 brown onions, peeled
4 cloves
3 leeks, coarsely chopped
60 g (2¼ oz) fresh ginger, peeled and finely chopped
2 lemongrass stems, pale part only, chopped
Bouquet garni
1 tablespoon coarse salt
6 pig tails
6 carrots, peeled and coarsely chopped
3 swedes (rutabagas), peeled and coarsely chopped
3 parsnips, peeled and coarsely chopped
Salt and pepper
3 tablespoons horseradish

**THE OXTAIL**
Blanching the oxtail removes any impurities. To blanch, place the oxtail pieces in a large saucepan of water. Bring to the boil. Drain, then rinse.

**THE POT-AU-FEU**
Stud the onions with the cloves.
Bring a large saucepan of water to the boil. Add the oxtail, onions, leek, ginger, lemongrass, bouquet garni and coarse salt. Bring to the boil then reduce the heat to low and simmer gently for 2 hours.
Add the pig tails, carrots, swedes and parsnips and cook for another 1½–2 hours, or until the tails are tender.
Season if necessary and serve with the broth and horseradish.

STAUB

# ROASTED PIG TAILS

**SERVES 6**
**20 MINUTES PREPARATION TIME**
**2 HOURS 15 MINUTES COOKING TIME**

6 pig tails
3 carrots, peeled
2 brown onions, peeled
1 fennel bulb
Bouquet garni
2 leeks
6 small parsnips (about 500 g/ 1 lb 2 oz), peeled
1 golden nugget pumpkin (winter squash), cut into wedges
100 ml (3½ fl oz) olive oil
3 lemons, cut into wedges
2 sweet salad onions, thinly sliced
Salt and pepper

**THE TAILS**
Place the pig tails, carrots, brown onions, fennel bulb, bouquet garni and leeks in a large saucepan. Cover with water. Bring to a simmer over a medium heat. Reduce the heat to low and simmer for 1 hour 45 minutes, or until the tails are tender.

**THE VEGETABLES**
Add the parsnips and pumpkin and continue cooking for 15 minutes.

**THE COOKING IN THE OVEN**
Preheat the oven grill (broiler) to medium–high.
Remove the tails, brown onions, parsnips and pumpkin from the cooking liquid. Coarsely chop the brown onions. Arrange the tails in a roasting tin with the chopped onion, parsnips and pumpkin. Drizzle with olive oil and squeeze over the lemon wedges.
Brown under the grill for 15 minutes. At serving time, add the sliced sweet onions, drizzle again with olive oil and season. Serve with the lemon wedges.

# LA JOUE

## CHEEK

**BEEF OR PORK CHEEK**
can be purchased from specialty butchers
may need to be ordered ahead of time
trim excess fat with a knife if necessary

## LATERAL SECTION OF THE HEAD OF CERTAIN ANIMALS

The cheek is one of the muscles that's highest in collagen. Its low fat content (cows chew a lot!) and rather long cooking time make it the ally of high-protein diets. Its tendonous tissues turn into gelatine over the course of several hours of simmering, giving cheeks their characteristic melting texture.

Beef cheek is the official representative of the boeuf bourguignon. Forget dry and stringy meats and permanently adopt one that will give character, succulence and tenderness to this very traditional dish. A good bourguignon made from beef cheeks will more than earn you two kisses on your own!

There's good to be found in tradition and the pig is its patron saint. Pig's cheeks, for their part, smile on the exotic and willingly team up with the spiciest ideas, lending spark to dishes full of charisma. Pigs have a cheekiness unlike their ruminating colleagues. They confit in lard, wake up in a curry and melt for our pleasure in a bath of rosemary. Sweet, spicy, or sweet-and-sour, pig's cheeks have an infinite palette of talents.

# BEEF CHEEK BOURGUIGNON

**SERVES 6**
**30 MINUTES PREPARATION TIME**
**3 HOURS COOKING TIME**

1 brown onion, peeled
2 cloves
1.2 kg (2 lb 10 oz) beef cheeks, trimmed of excess fat
50 g (1¾ oz) butter, chopped
2 tablespoons olive oil
200 g (7 oz) speck (smoked pork belly), cut into large lardons
2 tablespoons plain (all-purpose) flour
6 carrots, thickly sliced on the diagonal
Finely grated zest of 1 orange
2½ tablespoons Armagnac brandy
1 x 750 ml (26 fl oz) bottle of red wine, (Côtes du Rhône style works well)
1 pinch of ground cinnamon
Bouquet garni
Salt and pepper
500 g (1 lb 2 oz) cooked, peeled and vaccum-packed chestnuts (see note on page 20)
1 square of dark chocolate

**THE CHEEKS**

Stud the onion with the cloves. Cut the beef cheeks into cubes about 5 cm (2 inches) in size.

**COOKING**

Melt the butter with the olive oil in a flameproof casserole dish over a medium–high heat. Brown the beef cheek and speck for about 3–5 minutes, in batches. Return all the meat to the casserole dish then stir in the flour, carrot and orange zest. Flambé with the Armagnac then add the red wine, onion, cinnamon and the bouquet garni, and season. The meat should be covered with liquid so add some water if necessary. Bring to a simmer over a medium heat then reduce to low and simmer, covered, for 2–3 hours. Check how well the meat is cooked; it should be falling apart.

When ready to serve, warm the chestnuts in the bourguignon and add the dark chocolate to sweeten the sauce. Remove the onion, then serve.

# PRESSED BEEF CHEEK WITH VEGETABLES

**SERVES 6**
**20 MINUTES PREPARATION TIME**
**3 HOURS COOKING TIME**

- 800 g (1 lb 12 oz) beef cheeks, trimmed of excess fat
- 2 leeks, white part only, chopped
- 1 tablespoon coarse salt
- Bouquet garni
- 4 carrots, peeled and cut into 3 cm (1¼ inch) cubes
- 3 swedes, peeled and cut into 3 cm (1¼ inch) cubes
- ½ a celeriac, peeled and cut into 3 cm (1¼ inch) cubes
- 3 French shallots, finely chopped
- ½ a bunch of coriander (cilantro), leaves picked and chopped
- ½ a bunch of tarragon, leaves picked and chopped
- ½ a bunch of dill, finely chopped
- Salt and pepper
- 2 piquillo peppers, finely chopped
- 1 bunch of chives, finely chopped
- 150 ml (5 fl oz) olive oil

**THE CHEEKS**
Cut the beef cheeks into large cubes.

**COOKING**
Place the beef cheek, leek, coarse salt and the bouquet garni in a large saucepan of boiling water and simmer over a low heat for 2 hours. Add the carrot, swede and celeriac and continue cooking for 1 more hour, or until the pieces of beef cheek are falling apart and the vegetables are tender.
Remove the meat and vegetables from the cooking liquid. Discard the liquid, or save it for stock. Shred the meat and place it in a bowl with a third of the shallot and all of the coriander, tarragon and dill. Mix to combine then season.

**THE SAUCE**
For the sauce vierge, combine the remaining shallot with the peppers, chives, and olive oil in a bowl.

**ASSEMBLY**
Using food rings, layer the shredded meat mixture and cooked vegetables on serving plates. Press down firmly so it holds together then remove the rings. Serve lukewarm with the sauce vierge and a herb salad dressed with olive oil.

# CONFIT PORK CHEEKS

**SERVES 6**
**10 MINUTES PREPARATION TIME**
**2 HOURS COOKING TIME**

18 pork cheeks (about 2 kg/4 lb 8 oz), trimmed of excess fat
1 kg (2 lb 4 oz) lard, chopped
4 garlic cloves, peeled
3 sprigs of rosemary
1 bay leaf
1 teaspoon coarse salt
1 teaspoon cracked black pepper

**COOKING**
Put the pork cheeks in a large heavy-bottomed saucepan with the lard over a low heat. When the lard has completely melted, add the garlic, rosemary, bay leaf, coarse salt and pepper. Cook over a low heat, stirring at regular intervals so the meat doesn't catch on the bottom of the pan, for 2 hours. The meat should be soft and yield to the tip of a fork. Remove the cheeks from the lard and drain.

**HOW SHOULD I SERVE THEM?**
Warm, with tarragon mustard and steamed potatoes; or cold, in a salad with frisée lettuce and a well-flavoured mustard sauce.

**TIP**
The cheeks will keep in the fat in the fridge for several months. To store, place cheeks in an airtight container and cover completely with melted fat. Cool slightly then cover the container and refrigerate. To reheat, cook in a frying pan over a medium heat for 3–5 minutes, or until heated through.

# CURRIED PORK CHEEKS

**SERVES 6**
**45 MINUTES PREPARATION TIME**
**2 HOURS COOKING TIME**

- 50 g (1¾ oz) butter, chopped
- 2 tablespoons olive oil
- 18 pork cheeks (about 2 kg/4 lb 8 oz), trimmed of excess fat
- 1 tablespoon plain (all-purpose) flour
- 6 brown onions, peeled and chopped
- 3 carrots, peeled and sliced
- 2 celery stalks, thinly sliced
- 2 lemongrass stems, pale part only, thinly sliced
- 30 g (1 oz) fresh ginger, peeled and finely chopped
- 2 star anise
- 1 litre (35 fl oz/4 cups) dry white wine
- 2 teaspoons curry powder
- 1 pinch of saffron threads
- 20 baby onions
- 200 ml (7 fl oz) coconut milk
- Salt and pepper
- 12 basil leaves, thinly shredded

**COOKING**

Melt the butter with the olive oil in a flameproof casserole dish over a medium–high heat. Brown the pork cheeks, in batches, for 2–3 minutes. Return all the pork cheeks to the dish and stir in the flour.

Add the onion, carrot, celery, lemongrass, ginger, star anise, white wine, curry powder and saffron. Bring to the boil. Reduce the heat to low. Simmer, stirring occasionally, for 1½ hours, or until the pork is almost tender. Add the baby onions and coconut milk and cook for a further 30 minutes, stirring occasionally. Season.

Using a slotted spoon, transfer the meat and vegetables to a large bowl. Cover with foil to keep warm.

Transfer the cooking liquid to a blender, in batches, and mix until smooth. Return the sauce, meat and vegetables to the casserole dish, add the basil and serve immediately.

**SERVE WITH**

A good rice pilaf.

# PORK CHEEK RILLETTES

**MAKES 1 KG (2 LB 4 OZ) RILLETTES**
**15 MINUTES PREPARATION TIME**
**4 HOURS COOKING TIME**

- 400 g (14 oz) pork cheeks, trimmed of excess fat
- 300 g (10½ oz) fresh pork belly
- 250 g (9 oz/1 cup) lard
- 200 ml (7 fl oz) muscat sweet white wine (not fortified)
- 3 sprigs of rosemary
- 1 bay leaf
- 1 bunch of thyme
- 12 g (⅖ oz) salt
- 1 teaspoon Espelette chilli powder (or substitute with sweet paprika and chilli powder in a 3:1 ratio) (see note on page 24)

**THE CHEEKS**
Cut the pork cheeks and belly into 2 cm (¾ inch) cubes.

**COOKING**
Place the pork cheek, belly and the lard in a heavy-bottomed medium saucepan over a low heat. Once the lard has completely melted, add the wine, rosemary, bay leaf, thyme, salt and chilli powder. Cook, stirring at regular intervals so the meat doesn't catch on the bottom of the pan, for 4 hours, or until the meat is falling apart.

**THE RILLETTES**
Carefully take the meat out of the pan and transfer to a board. Shred with two forks and adjust the seasoning if necessary. Pack the rillettes tightly into small sterilised, airtight jars and cover with the strained melted lard. Seal and serve at room temperature.

**TIP**
Rillettes keep for several weeks in the refrigerator. Ideal for friends who drop in unexpectedly!

# PROVENÇAL STUFFED VEGETABLES

**SERVES 6**
**30 MINUTES PREPARATION TIME**
**40 MINUTES COOKING TIME**

6 small round zucchini (courgettes) (see note)
6 small brown onions, unpeeled
½ a bunch of parsley
½ a bunch of basil
500 g (1 lb 2 oz) confit pork cheeks (see recipe on page 124)
4 garlic cloves, finely chopped
1 teaspoon ground cinnamon
1 teaspoon ground cumin
1 teaspoon fennel seeds
2 tablespoons finely grated parmesan cheese
Salt and pepper
Olive oil

**THE VEGETABLES**

Slice the lids off the top of the zucchini and onions and trim their bases so they stand upright. Scoop out their insides with a melon baller or teaspoon, leaving a 5 mm (¼ inch) border.

**THE STUFFING**

Finely chop the zucchini and onion flesh with the parsley and basil and transfer to a bowl. Shred the pork cheek meat and add it to the zucchini mixture with the garlic, cinnamon, cumin, fennel seeds and parmesan. Mix to combine and season.

**COOKING**

Preheat the oven to 180°C (350°F/Gas 4).
Stuff each vegetable with some filling then top with the lid. Place on baking trays, drizzle with a little olive oil and bake for 35–40 minutes, or until the vegetables are tender.

**NOTE**

If round zucchini are unavailable, you can either substitute with medium-sized long zucchini or similar-sized round vegetables such as small pumpkins (winter squash), but you may need to adjust cooking times accordingly.

# LA LANGUE

## TONGUE

**BEEF, VEAL, PORK OR LAMB TONGUE**
can be purchased from specialty butchers
may need to be ordered ahead of time
blanch and rinse before cooking

## FLESHY, ELONGATED MUSCLE, LOCATED IN THE ORAL CAVITY OF ANIMALS

Beef and veal tongue start talking as soon as the green pokes through the concrete and the paths are no longer covered with snow; as soon as the living gets easy. These vernacular tongues have a regional flavour, with a particular accent on protein and fat, and are a source of vitamin B12, their local idiom. Delicate in style, tongues were long reserved for lords before being democratised to become the *lingua franca* they are today, found in every continent.

They're ebullient boiled, conversational in salads, opinionated in a pot-au-feu, and chatty with whoever pays them heed. Veal tongue, especially, lends itself to being rolled in the head. Lamb tongue and pork tongue are more discreet, more confidential. Lamb tongue is no doubt the most prized and deserves the most attention. It combines finesse and character with an oriental inflection when it runs into Lebanon, and an exotic lilt in Morocco; this cosmopolitan tongue is universal. Pork tongue, properly speaking, is rarely spoken. It is often a dead tongue preserved in brine or combined with others to form a patois called head cheese. There is no place, in any case, for the *langue de bois* here.

# BEEF TONGUE WITH CAPERS

**SERVES 6**
**20 MINUTES PREPARATION TIME**
**3 HOURS 15 MINUTES COOKING TIME**

- 1 beef tongue
- 3 carrots, peeled and thickly sliced
- 3 brown onions, thickly sliced
- 2 celery stalks, thickly sliced
- Bouquet garni
- 30 g (1 oz) butter, chopped
- 2 French shallots, finely chopped
- 1 teaspoon plain (all-purpose) flour
- 100 ml (3½ fl oz) tawny port
- 2 tomatoes, well-ripened, diced
- 2 medium zucchini (courgettes), halved lengthways and sliced
- 12 cornichons, cut into matchsticks
- 1 tablespoon capers, rinsed
- 200 ml (7 fl oz) thin (pouring) cream
- Salt and pepper

**THE TONGUE**

Boil the tongue in a large saucepan of boiling water for 5 minutes. Remove the scum from the top and rinse well.

**COOKING**

Fill a saucepan with cold water and add the tongue, carrot, onion, celery and the bouquet garni. Bring to a simmer over a medium heat then reduce the heat to low. Cook for 3 hours. The meat should be very tender.
Take the tongue out of the cooking liquid, remove the skin and cut the meat into thin slices. Keep these warm in the cooking liquid.

**THE SAUCE**

Melt the butter in a frying pan over a medium heat and add the shallot. Cook, stirring occasionally, until softened then add the flour and mix well with a whisk. Add the port, a glass of the cooking liquid, the tomato, zucchini, cornichon and capers. After cooking for 5 minutes, add the cream and gently reduce until the sauce coats the back of a spoon. Season.
Arrange the slices of tongue on a plate, spoon over the vegetables and sauce and serve immediately.

# VEAL TONGUE SALAD

**SERVES 6**
**30 MINUTES PREPARATION TIME**
**2 HOURS COOKING TIME**

3 veal tongues
3 carrots, thickly sliced
3 brown onions, thickly sliced
2 celery stalks, thickly sliced
Bouquet garni
100 g (3½ oz/⅔ cup) fresh shelled peas
1 tablespoon wholegrain mustard
1 tablespoon Melfor vinegar (see note)
2 tablespoons canola oil
2 tablespoons olive oil
Salt and pepper
2 sweet salad onions or bulb spring onions (scallions), thinly sliced
4 tomatoes, seeded, thinly sliced
6 artichokes in oil, drained and thinly sliced
2 zucchini (courgettes), halved lengthways and thinly sliced
1 bunch of dill, leaves picked

**THE TONGUES**
Boil the tongues in a saucepan of boiling water for 5 minutes. Drain and rinse well.

**COOKING**
Fill a saucepan with cold water. Add the tongue, carrot, brown onion, celery and bouquet garni. Cook over a low heat for 2 hours. The meat should be very tender. Remove the tongue from the saucepan, peel and discard the skin and cut the meat into thin slices. Transfer to a large bowl. Discard the cooking liquid and vegetables.

**THE SALAD**
Drop the peas into boiling salted water for 3 minutes and refresh immediately in cold water so they retain their colour. Drain then add to the meat. Whisk the mustard, Melfor vinegar and canola and olive oils in a bowl then season. Toss all of the ingredients together in the dressing and serve immediately.

**NOTE**
Melfor vinegar is a honey vinegar from the Alsace region of France. If not available from specialty suppliers, substitute with good-quality apple cider vinegar or white balsamic vinegar.

# LAMB TONGUE FRICASSÉE

**SERVES 6**
**30 MINUTES PREPARATION TIME**
**2 HOURS 15 MINS COOKING TIME**

6 lamb tongues
3 carrots, thickly sliced
3 brown onions, thickly sliced
2 celery stalks, thickly sliced
Bouquet garni
400 g (14 oz) fresh chanterelle mushrooms (see note)
50 g (1¾ oz) butter
3 bulb spring onions (scallions), quartered lengthways
1 bunch of tarragon, leaves picked
200 g (7 oz) cooked, peeled and vacuum-packed chestnuts (see note on page 20)
100 ml (3½ fl oz) sake
2 tablespoons soy sauce
200 g (7 oz) bean sprouts, trimmed
Pepper

**THE TONGUES**

Boil the tongues in a saucepan of boiling water for 5 minutes. Drain and rinse well.

**COOKING**

Fill a saucepan with cold water. Add the tongues, carrot, brown onion, celery and the bouquet garni. Bring to a simmer over a medium heat then reduce the heat to low. Cook for 2 hours. The meat should be very tender. Remove the meat from the cooking liquid. Peel and discard the skin and cut the meat into very thin slices. Discard the cooking liquid and vegetables.

**THE FRICASSÉE**

Gently clean the mushrooms with a clean damp cloth or paper towels. Melt the butter in a wok over a medium–high heat then sauté the sliced tongue and spring onions for 5 minutes. Add the mushrooms, tarragon and chestnuts and sauté for 5 minutes, or until softened. Deglaze the wok with the sake then add the soy sauce and bean sprouts. Sauté for another 5 minutes, season with pepper and serve immediately.

**NOTE**

Chanterelle mushrooms are seasonal. Purchase fresh from specialty French food or mushroom suppliers. If unavailable, use fresh pine or Swiss brown mushrooms.

# SMOKY PORK TONGUES

**SERVES 6**
**15 MINUTES PREPARATION TIME**
**3 HOURS COOKING TIME**

3 pork tongues
1 end piece of prosciutto
200 g (7 oz) speck (smoked pork belly)
6 leeks, white part only, coarsely chopped
4 brown onions, coarsely chopped
4 celery stalks, coarsely chopped
Bouquet garni
1 tablespoon cumin seeds
Salt and pepper

**THE TONGUES**
Boil the tongues in a saucepan of boiling water for 5 minutes. Drain and rinse well.

**COOKING**
Place all of the ingredients in a large saucepan, season then fill the saucepan with cold water. Bring to a simmer over a medium heat then reduce the heat to low. Cook for 2 hours, the meat should be very tender.
Remove the meat from the cooking liquid. Discard the piece of prosciutto. Peel and discard the skin from the tongues then cut the tongues in half lengthways. Chop the speck into big, thick lardons. Transfer to a bowl and cover to keep warm.
Reduce the cooking liquid by a third. Reheat the tongue and speck in the cooking liquid for a few minutes. Serve immediately.

**TIP**
Don't forget to 'faire chabrot' to finish the meal by adding a little red wine to the broth in your plate!

# LA CERVELLE

## BRAINS

**CALF, LAMB OR PIG BRAINS**
can be purchased from some supermarkets or specialty butchers
may need to be ordered ahead of time
soak in vinegared water for 10 minutes

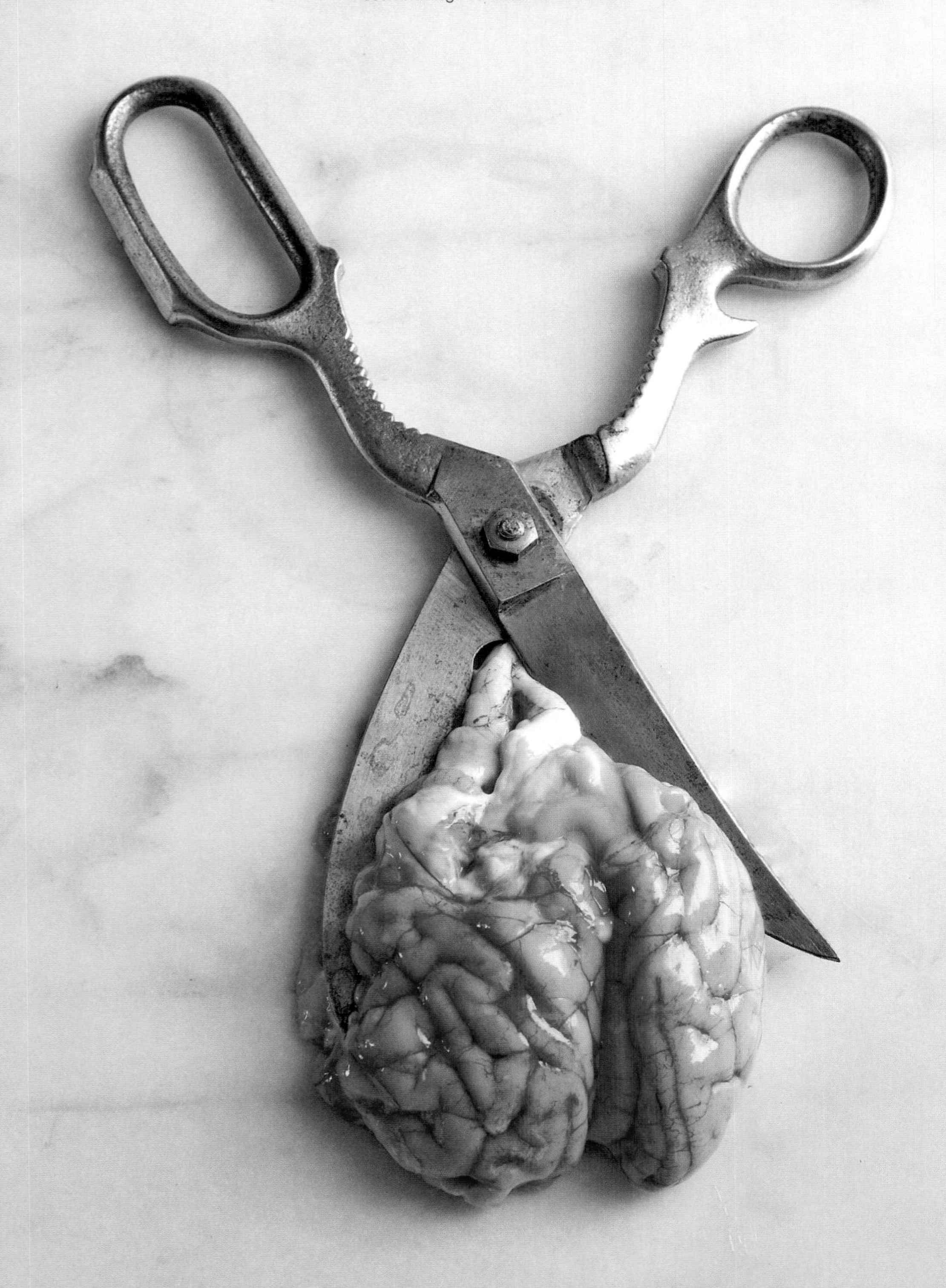

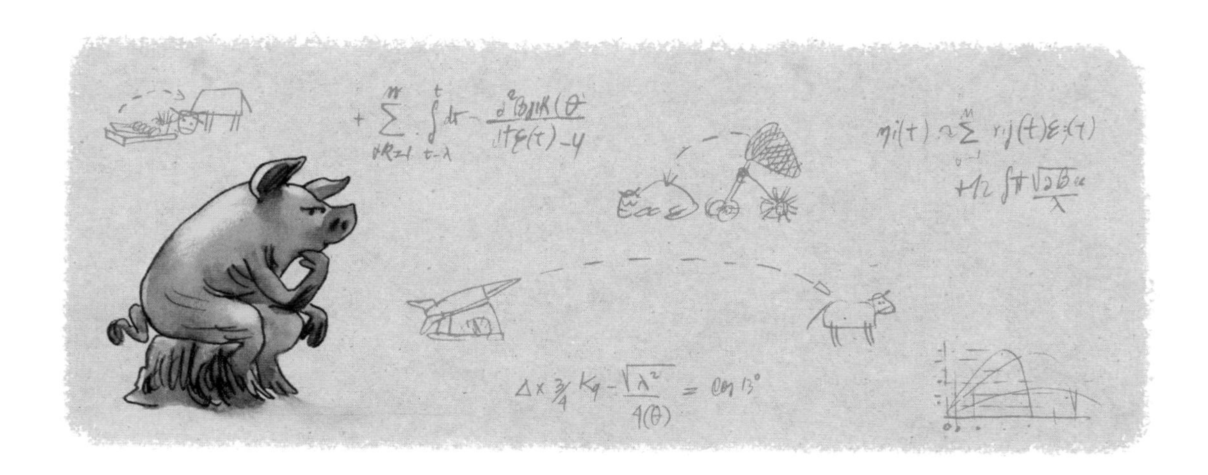

## THE BRAIN OF CERTAIN ANIMALS, SERVED AS FOOD

When you think about it, the brain is really the most unlikely part of the animal to consume. These beasts play host to so much pointless thought, hot air, incomprehensible bleating, inaudible grunting, meaningless gestures, faux pas, animality, inappropriate displays and chronic incontinence, that it seems unthinkable to savour the engine room of everything just mentioned. But fear not, there is no risk of contagion, and if, God forbid, you encounter some of the abovementioned symptoms in a member of your party, it's because they're an idiot, and nothing can be done for them. Brains are the least profitable offal meat from a nutritional point of view. Apart from vitamin B12 and phosphorus (useful for sparkling), they are in effect very high in cholesterol — being too brainy can make you sick! If buying, calf or lamb brains are recommended; they should be pale in colour and lightly veined, with a pleasant smell. Brains need to soak for a few hours in cold salted water to remove any traces of blood. They can be poached, pan-fried, deep-fried or braised to make a memorable meal.

# LAMB BRAINS MEUNIÈRE

**SERVES 6**
**10 MINUTES PREPARATION TIME**
**15 MINUTES COOKING TIME**

6 lamb brains
60 ml (2 fl oz/¼ cup) white vinegar
2 tablespoons plain (all-purpose) flour
100 g (3½ oz) butter, chopped
2 tablespoons sunflower oil
Salt and pepper

**THE BRAINS**
Soak the brains for 10 minutes in a bowl of water with half of the vinegar. Drain then rinse carefully and gently remove any membranes enveloping them.
Poach the brains for 5 minutes in a saucepan of simmering water with the remaining vinegar. Rinse and thoroughly pat dry with paper towels.

**COOKING**
Place the flour in a shallow bowl and dust the brains.
Melt 40 g (1½ oz) of the butter with the sunflower oil in a large frying pan over a medium heat. Brown the brains for 5 minutes then keep warm in front of a lit oven.
Wash the frying pan and make a beurre noisette with the remaining butter by cooking it over a medium heat, swirling often, until the butter turns a nut-brown colour.
Toss the brains in this butter until reheated then season and serve immediately.

**SERVE WITH**
Steamed potatoes.

# CALF BRAINS WITH LEMON AND CROUTONS

**SERVES 6**
**20 MINUTES PREPARATION TIME**
**25 MINUTES COOKING TIME**

3 calf brains
60 ml (2 fl oz/¼ cup) white vinegar
4 slices of sandwich bread, diced
3 tablespoons plain (all-purpose) flour
100 g (3½ oz) butter, chopped
2 tablespoons sunflower oil
2 tablespoons capers, rinsed
2 lemons, peeled and segmented
1 bunch of chives, snipped
Salt and pepper

**THE BRAINS**
Soak the brains for 10 minutes in a bowl of water with half of the vinegar. Drain then rinse carefully and gently remove any membranes enveloping them.
Poach the brains for 10 minutes in a saucepan of simmering water with the remaining vinegar. Rinse and thoroughly pat dry with paper towels.

**THE LEMONS AND CROUTONS**
Preheat the oven to 180°C (350°F/Gas 4). Place the diced bread on a baking tray and bake for 5 minutes, or until they're nice and crunchy.

**COOKING**
Place the flour in a shallow bowl. Cut the brains into large cubes and dust lightly in the flour. Melt 40 g (1½ oz) of the butter with the sunflower oil in a large frying pan over a medium heat. Brown the brains on all sides for 5 minutes. Keep the brains warm in front of a lit oven.
Wash the frying pan and make a beurre noisette with the remaining butter by cooking it over a medium heat, swirling often, until the butter turns a nut-brown colour.
Toss the brains in this beurre noisette and add the croutons, capers, lemon segments and chives. Season and serve.

**SERVE WITH**
A dish of green beans with garlic.

# PEPPERED BRAIN FRITTERS

**SERVES 6**
**20 MINUTES PREPARATION TIME**
**15 MINUTES COOKING TIME**

4 pig brains
60 ml (2 fl oz/¼ cup) white vinegar
1 garlic clove, finely chopped
1 tablespoon herbes de Provence (mixed dried herbs)
50 g (1¾ oz) butter, chopped
150 g (5½ oz/1 cup) plain (all-purpose) flour
4 eggs
Salt
1 tablespoon cracked black pepper
Vegetable oil, for deep-frying
4 green cabbage leaves from the centre, thinly shredded
60 ml (2 fl oz/¼ cup) olive oil
1 tablespoon rice vinegar

**THE BRAINS**
Soak the brains for 10 minutes in a bowl of water with half of the white vinegar. Drain then rinse carefully and gently remove any membranes enveloping them. Poach the brains for 5 minutes in a saucepan of simmering water with the remaining vinegar. Rinse and thoroughly pat dry with paper towels.

**THE FRITTER BATTER**
Bring 400 ml (14 fl oz) of water to the boil in a saucepan with the garlic, herbs and butter. Add the flour and stir with a spatula until the mixture comes away from the side of the saucepan. Remove from the heat and cool slightly. Add the eggs one at a time, stirring until combined. Season with salt.

**COOKING**
Quarter the brains. Dip them in the batter and sprinkle with cracked pepper. Add enough vegetable oil to a large saucepan to reach a depth of 10 cm (4 inches). Heat it to 180°C (350°F) and deep-fry the brains, in batches, for 5 minutes, or until golden brown. Drain on paper towels. Serve with a green cabbage salad dressed with the olive oil and rice vinegar.

# LA TÊTE

## HEAD

**WHOLE CALF'S HEAD:** boned, skin removed and rolled around the skinned tongue by the butcher
order from specialty butchers ahead of time

**WHOLE PIG'S HEAD:** ready to cook
order from specialty butchers ahead of time

**PIG'S EAR:** ready to cook
order from specialty butchers ahead of time

**PIG'S SNOUT:** ready to cook
order from specialty butchers ahead of time

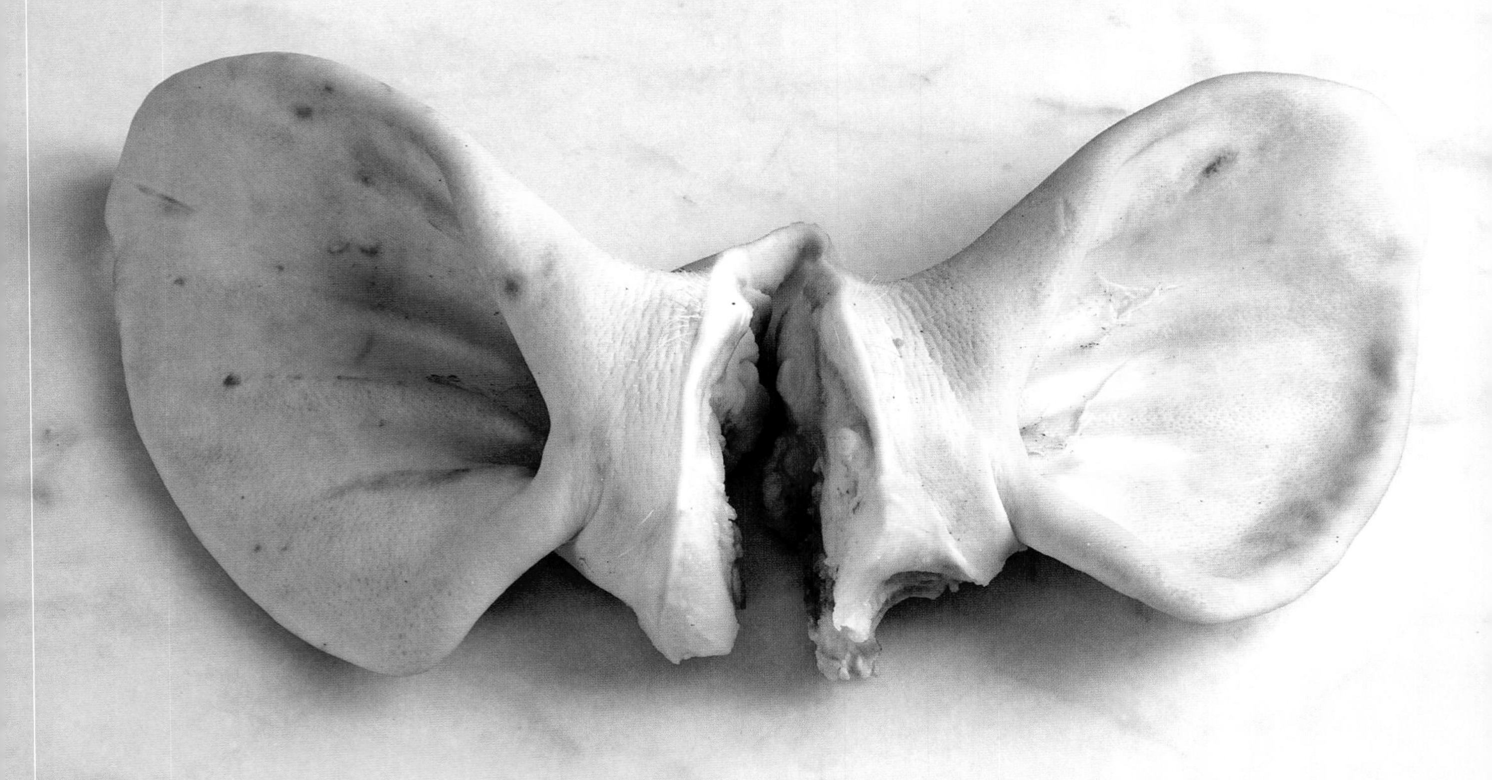

# THE ANTERIOR END OF MANY ANIMALS, CONTAINING THE TONGUE, BRAIN AND MAIN SENSORY ORGANS

Eat a head. Now there's a preposterous idea for a lover of fine flesh. The famous butcher Guillotin, who had a good head on his shoulders, propelled this repellent dish headfirst into the firmament of cuisine. Calf or pig, the choice is yours… Calf's head, *tête de veau*, generally comes boned and rolled with the tongue in the middle. It is shaped like a large sausage wrapped in fishnet mesh. This ageing-stripper get-up will hold the meats together during cooking. Calf's head must be served meltingly tender, it is eaten with a spoon, accompanied by a sauce ravigote or gribiche. For two five-year terms, calf's head reigned over presidential dinners in France, much to the despair of visiting heads of state.

Whole pig's head is mainly used for making *fromage de tête* (head cheese), a strange name for a fresh dish eaten at the beginning of the meal. The etymology of this name is derived, according to knowledgeable male sources, from a quarrel between the butcher Guillotin and his assistant Neuneuil. After Neuneuil had overcooked a pig's head in stock, he decided to chop up the meat with parsley and form it into a terrine, pouring over the cooking liquid. Guillotin had a rush of blood to the head, but Neuneuil held on to his: 'What are you making such a fuss about, big cheese?' Guillotin turned the dish to his advantage and put up a sign in his shop, head held high: 'Head cheese, 3 germinal francs per pound'. It was an instant success.

# TÊTE DE VEAU CLASSIQUE

**SERVES 6**
**30 MINUTES PREPARATION TIME**
**3 HOURS 10 MINUTES COOKING TIME**

1 rolled calf's head with its tongue, prepared by the butcher
3 leeks, white parts only, sliced
3 brown onions, peeled
1 round savoy cabbage, cut into 6 wedges
Bouquet garni
1 tablespoon coarse salt
6 waxy potatoes such as charlotte or desiree, peeled
6 carrots, peeled
2 tablespoons dijon mustard
1 tablespoon white wine vinegar
200 ml (7 fl oz) olive oil
3 eggs, hard-boiled, peeled and chopped
1 bunch of chives, finely chopped
3 bulb spring onions (scallions), finely chopped
Fine sea salt and pepper
3 pig brains, prepared by the butcher

**THE HEAD**
Fill a large saucepan with water. Add the calf's head, leek, brown onions, cabbage, bouquet garni and coarse salt. Bring to a simmer over a medium heat. Reduce the heat to low and simmer for 2½ hours, or until the meat is tender. Add the potatoes and carrots and continue cooking for another 30 minutes.

**THE SAUCE**
Meanwhile, in a bowl mix the mustard and vinegar. Emulsify with the olive oil, whisking vigorously until combined. Add the eggs, chives and spring onion then season. Mix until combined then set the sauce aside.

**THE BRAINS**
Remove the meat and vegetables from the cooking liquid once cooked and place in a bowl, covered, to keep warm. Return the saucepan to a medium heat and poach the pig brains in the cooking liquid for 10 minutes. Remove and drain.
Cut the head into slices and serve with the cooked vegetables and brains. Spoon over the sauce at the last minute, sprinkle with sea salt and serve.

# CRUNCHY CALF'S HEAD

**SERVES 6**
**20 MINUTES PREPARATION TIME**
**3 HOURS 20 MINUTES COOKING TIME**
**1 HOUR CHILLING TIME**

- 1 rolled calf's head with its tongue, prepared by the butcher
- 3 leeks, halved
- 6 brown onions, peeled
- Bouquet garni
- 1 tablespoon coarse salt
- 8 waxy potatoes such as charlotte or desiree, peeled
- 2 tomatoes, well-ripened
- 1 celery stalk, finely chopped
- 3 bulb spring onions (scallions), finely chopped
- 1 bunch of chives, finely chopped
- 200 ml (7 fl oz) olive oil, plus extra for drizzling
- 3 eggs, lightly whisked
- Salt and pepper
- 12 medium French toast crackers, finely crushed

**THE POACHING**

Place the calf's head, leeks, 3 brown onions, bouquet garni and coarse salt into a large saucepan. Cover with water. Bring to the boil over a medium heat. Reduce the heat to low. Simmer for 2½ hours, or until the meat is tender. Add the potatoes and cook for a further 30 minutes. Remove and drain the head and potatoes. Chill the head for 1 hour.

**THE ACCOMPANIMENTS**

Meanwhile, drop the tomatoes into boiling water for 10 seconds then drain them, allow to cool and peel their skins. Cut the flesh into small cubes. Transfer to a bowl with the celery, spring onion, chives and half of the olive oil. Combine then set aside. Preheat the oven grill (broiler) to medium–high. Thinly slice the remaining brown onions. Add to a roasting dish with the potatoes, mix together and season. Drizzle with olive oil and grill for 15–20 minutes, or until golden brown. Remove and lightly crush the potatoes.

**CRUMBING AND COOKING**

Preheat the oven to 180°C (350°F/Gas 4). Place the whisked egg in a shallow bowl and season. Place the cracker crumbs in another shallow bowl. Cut the head into 2 cm (¾ inch) thick slices. Dip the slices in the egg, then in the crumbs, pressing firmly to evenly coat.
Fry the slices, in batches, in the remaining olive oil over a medium–high heat for 3 minutes on each side, or until golden. Finish them in the oven for 5–10 minutes, or until hot through.
To serve, mash and shape the potato and onion mixture into patties, place a slice of calf's head on top, drizzle over the sauce and serve immediately.

# PÂTÉ DE TÊTE

**MAKES 1 X 1.2 KG (2 LB 10 OZ) TERRINE**
**30 MINUTES PREPARATION TIME**
**4 HOURS COOKING TIME**
**1 DAY CHILLING TIME**

3 brown onions, peeled
6 cloves
1 pig's head (remove hairs with a clean razor if necessary) (see note)
1 calf's foot, halved
4 pork cheeks
4 leeks, peeled
3 celery stalks
Bouquet garni
1 generous tablespoon coarse salt
4 carrots, peeled
2 French shallots, finely chopped
1 bunch of parsley, leaves picked, finely chopped
Salt and pepper

### THE POACHING

Stud the brown onions with the cloves and place in a large stockpot with the pig's head, calf's foot, pork cheeks, leeks, celery, bouquet garni and coarse salt. Cover with water and bring to a simmer over a medium heat. Reduce the heat to low and simmer for 3 hours. Add the carrots and cook for 1 more hour.

### THE AROMATICS

Take the head, foot and cheeks out of the water and put aside to drain and cool. Remove the carrots and celery. Reserve the cooking liquid. When cool enough to handle, bone the head, discarding everything except the meat. Finely chop all of the meat and the carrots and celery. Combine everything with the shallot and parsley and season well. Strain the cooking liquid through a muslin-lined strainer into a large saucepan. Discard any solids.

### THE PÂTÉ

Fill a 1.5 litre (52 fl oz/6 cup) capacity terrine dish or loaf (bar) tin with the pâté mixture. Pack it down well to avoid air bubbles. Cover completely with the strained cooking liquid (gently tapping the dish on the work surface to help remove any remaining air bubbles). Cover tightly with plastic wrap and refrigerate for 24 hours. The terrine will keep for 2 weeks in the refrigerator. To serve, turn out and serve with pickled cocktail onions and pickled cherries or caperberries and toasted bread. Consume the same day.

### NOTE

If you don't think you have a pot large enough to fit a whole pig's head, ask the butcher to chop the head in half lengthways for you.

ville

# GRILLED PIG EARS

**SERVES 6**
**5 MINUTES PREPARATION TIME**
**1 HOUR 15 MINUTES COOKING TIME**

1 brown onion, peeled
2 cloves
6 pig ears, prepared by the butcher
4 carrots, sliced into rounds
1 celery stalk
Bouquet garni
1 leek
120 ml (3¾ fl oz) sweet soy sauce
1 tablespoon herbes de Provence (mixed dried herbs)
Fine sea salt

### POACHING THE EARS

Stud the onion with the cloves and place in a large saucepan with the pig ears, carrot, celery, bouquet garni and leek. Cover with water. Bring to a simmer over a medium heat. Reduce the heat to low and simmer for 1 hour, or until the ears are tender. Remove and drain the ears and arrange them on a baking tray lined with baking paper.

### GRILLING THE EARS

Preheat the oven grill (broiler) to medium.
Using a pastry brush, glaze the ears with the sweet soy sauce, sprinkle with the herbs and season with sea salt. Place under the hot grill for 15 minutes, turning the ears halfway through the cooking time.

### HOW SHOULD I SERVE THEM?

As an entrée, with a potato salad.

# PIG EARS WITH FRESH HERBS

**SERVES 6**
**20 MINUTES PREPARATION TIME**
**1 HOUR 15 MINUTES COOKING TIME**

1 brown onion, peeled
2 cloves
4 pig ears, prepared by the butcher
4 carrots, sliced into rounds
1 celery stalk
Bouquet garni
1 leek
1 tablespoon coarse salt
2 tablespoons olive oil
3 bulb spring onions (scallions), finely chopped
4 tomatoes, seeded and thinly sliced
12 sun-dried tomatoes in oil, drained and coarsely chopped
50 g (1¾ oz/⅓ cup) pine nuts, toasted
Salt and pepper
½ a bunch of tarragon, leaves picked
½ a bunch of dill, leaves picked
½ a bunch of chervil, leaves picked
Frisée lettuce salad, to serve (optional)

**POACHING THE EARS**
Stud the onion with the cloves and place in a large saucepan with the pig ears, carrot, celery, bouquet garni, leek and salt. Cover with water. Bring to a simmer over a medium heat. Reduce the heat to low. Simmer for 1 hour, or until the ears are tender. Remove the ears from the cooking liquid and set aside to cool. Discard the cooking liquid, bouquet garni and vegetables.

**THE SALAD**
Cut the ears into thick strips and sauté in the olive oil over a medium–high heat with the spring onion. Cook, stirring occasionally, for 5 minutes, or until browned then add the sliced tomato, sun-dried tomato and pine nuts. Season and cook, stirring occasionally, until the vegetables have softened.
When ready to serve, scatter over the herb leaves and accompany with a good frisée lettuce salad.

# PIG SNOUTS WITH WALNUT OIL

**SERVES 6**
**25 MINUTES PREPARATION TIME**
**1 HOUR COOKING TIME**

1 brown onion, peeled
2 cloves
3 pig snouts, prepared by the butcher
4 carrots, halved lengthways
1 celery stalk
Bouquet garni
1 leek
1 tablespoon coarse salt
1 tablespoon dijon mustard
1 tablespoon white wine vinegar
2 tablespoons walnut oil
2 tablespoons sunflower oil
1 French shallot, finely chopped
12 cornichons, cut into long, thin slices
Salt and pepper
2 tablespoons pickled cocktail onions
1 bunch of flat-leaf (Italian) parsley, leaves picked

**THE SNOUTS**
Stud the onion with the cloves and place in a large saucepan with the pig snouts, carrot, celery, bouquet garni, leek and salt. Cover with water. Bring to a simmer over a medium heat. Reduce the heat to low and simmer for 1 hour, or until the pig snouts are tender. Remove the snouts from the cooking liquid and thinly slice. Remove the carrots from the cooking liquid and slice on the diagonal. Discard the cooking liquid, remaining vegetables and the bouquet garni.

**THE DRESSING**
Make a vinaigrette with the mustard, vinegar, walnut and sunflower oils and shallot. Combine the sliced meat, carrots and cornichons with the vinaigrette. Serve with the pickled onions and parsley leaves.

# LES PIÈCES DU BOUCHER
## BUTCHER'S CUTS

**POPE'S EYE (SPIDER STEAK):** ready to cook
order ahead of time from a specialty butcher

**HANGER STEAK:** ready to cook

**SKIRT STEAK:** ready to cook

**MARROW BONES:** ready to cook

**SPINAL CORD:** ready to cook
beef and lamb spinal cord can be purchased from specialty butchers
order ahead of time

## VERY TASTY CUTS OF MEAT, OBTURATOR AND DIAPHRAGM MUSCLES

Here are the cuts of meat called butcher's cuts. Pope's eye or 'spider steak', hanger and skirt steak are often the pieces that the butcher discreetly sets aside for his private consumption. None of these cuts weighs more than 700 g (1 lb 9 oz) — enough to serve two good eaters (the butcher and his wife). These pieces are considered to be the tastiest, with an incomparable texture. You have to be on intimate terms (so to speak) with your butcher to nourish a hope of dining on a nice juicy pope's eye.

Today, these cuts are mostly found in bistros, which know how to make the most of their gastronomic qualities. Shallots make light of hanger steak, marrow bones dance with skirt, pope's eyes swoon with butter-enriched jus. Unfortunately, French production can't meet demand and we have to import pope's eye, hanger and skirt steak to satisfy our appetites for them. These cuts are seared in butter and browned just enough to caramelise the surface and lock the juices inside. The same juices that soon, under the impact of hungry teeth, will spread their mellow charm over our impatient palates. It's a succulent experience, the meat rolls around the mouth like a good wine, you forget yourself…

You don't forget yourself too much, though, because back at the butcher's shop, other treasures remain tucked out of sight and you'll need your most winning smile if you want to see them in your basket. Bone marrow is the gentle heart of the beast; it makes your taste buds weep. By itself or in a pot-au-feu, it adds that dash of wow that makes all the difference. And what can we say about the spinal cord? It has the disturbing appearance of a large and slithering worm, but is so terribly toothsome…

# POPE'S EYE WITH PARSLEY BUTTER

**SERVES 6**
**20 MINUTES PREPARATION TIME**
**10 MINUTES COOKING TIME**

- 100 g (3½ oz) butter, chopped and softened
- 1 bulb spring onion (scallion), coarsely chopped
- 1 French shallot, coarsely chopped
- 2 garlic cloves, finely chopped
- ¼ bunch of parsley, coarsely chopped
- Salt and freshly ground black pepper
- 1 tablespoon sunflower oil
- 6 × 170 g (6 oz) pope's eye steaks

**THE PARSLEY BUTTER**
Combine the butter, spring onion, shallot, garlic and parsley in a bowl. Season.

**THE POPE'S EYES**
Melt half of the parsley butter in a large frying pan with the sunflower oil over a high heat and sear the pope's eye steaks, in batches, over a high heat.
Transfer to a plate, cover with foil and rest for 5 minutes.
Melt the rest of the butter in the frying pan and scrape up any bits from the bottom of the pan.
Thinly slice the pope's eye steaks and spoon over the parsley butter.

**SERVE WITH**
Home-made chips (fries).

# GRILLED POPE'S EYE AND SHIITAKE MUSHROOMS

**SERVES 6**
**15 MINUTES PREPARATION TIME**
**10 MINUTES COOKING TIME**

800 g (1 lb 12 oz) shiitake mushrooms
100 ml (3½ fl oz) olive oil
4 bulb spring onions (scallions), whites finely chopped, greens thinly sliced
Salt and pepper
100 g (3½ oz) butter, chopped
1 tablespoon sunflower oil
6 × 170 g (6 oz) pope's eye steaks
100 ml (3½ fl oz) dry white wine

**THE SHIITAKE MUSHROOMS**
Clean the mushrooms with a damp cloth and trim the stems. Heat the olive oil in a large frying pan over a medium heat. Add the mushrooms and chopped whites of the spring onions and sauté for 10 minutes, stirring occasionally, or until softened. Season.

**THE POPE'S EYES**
Meanwhile, melt half of the butter with the sunflower oil in another large frying pan over a high heat and sear the steaks in batches. Adjust the cooking time for individual tastes. Transfer to a plate, cover with foil and rest for 5 minutes.

Deglaze the frying pan used for the steaks with the white wine and reduce. Add the sliced greens of the spring onions and the remaining butter. Whisk everything together.

Serve the steaks with the mushrooms, drizzle with the butter from the pan and season.

# HANGER STEAK WITH SHALLOTS

**SERVES 6**
**15 MINUTES PREPARATION TIME**
**20 MINUTES COOKING TIME**

6 banana shallots, unpeeled
100 g (3½ oz) butter
1 tablespoon sunflower oil
1.2 kg (2 lb 10 oz) hanger steak, membrane and sinew removed by the butcher
Salt and pepper
2½ tablespoons Cognac brandy
3 carrots, very finely diced
1 celery stalk, very finely diced
200 ml (7 fl oz) veal stock
1 teaspoon tomato paste (concentrated purée)

**THE VEGETABLES**
Preheat the oven to 180°C (350°F/Gas 4). Bake the shallots for 20 minutes then halve lengthways.

**THE HANGER STEAK**
Meanwhile, melt half of the butter with the sunflower oil in a large frying pan over a high heat. Sear the hanger steak and cook for 5–10 minutes (for very rare), or to the desired level of doneness, turning occasionally until browned. Season. Transfer to a plate, cover with foil and rest for 10 minutes.

**THE VEGETABLE JUS**
Deglaze the frying pan with the brandy, flambé the brandy and add the diced vegetables, veal stock and tomato paste. Cook, stirring occasionally, for 5 minutes, or until the vegetables have softened. Remove from the heat, add the remaining butter and whisk.
Cut the hanger steak into slices. Divide between serving plates, spoon over the vegetable jus, top each serve with a halved shallot and serve immediately.

# PAN-FRIED HANGER STEAK WITH HERB SALAD

**SERVES 6**
**20 MINUTES PREPARATION TIME**
**10 MINUTES COOKING TIME**

- 100 g (3½ oz/2¼ cups) baby spinach
- 100 g (3½ oz) baby mustard greens or rocket (arugula)
- 2 carrots, peeled, cut into thin matchsticks
- 2 bulb spring onions (scallions), cut into thin matchsticks
- 1 teaspoon cumin seeds
- 2 tablespoons rice vinegar
- 1 tablespoon Maggi seasoning sauce
- 80 ml (2½ fl oz/⅓ cup) olive oil
- 1 teaspoon cracked black pepper
- 50 g (1¾ oz) butter, chopped
- 1 tablespoon sunflower oil
- 1.2 kg (2 lb 10 oz) hanger steak, membrane and sinew removed by the butcher
- Salt and cracked black pepper

**THE HERB SALAD**

Combine the salad leaves in a bowl with the carrot, spring onion and cumin seeds.
Make a vinaigrette by mixing together the rice vinegar, seasoning sauce, olive oil and pepper.

**THE HANGER STEAK**

Melt the butter with the sunflower oil in a large frying pan over a high heat. Sear the hanger steak and cook for 5–10 minutes (for very rare), or to the desired level of doneness, turning occasionally until browned. Season. Transfer to a plate, cover with foil and rest for 5 minutes. Cut the hanger steak into six even-sized portions. Divide between serving plates. Toss the salad with the dressing and serve immediately with the steak.

# SKIRT STEAK WITH PARSLEY PURÉE

**SERVES 6**
**20 MINUTES PREPARATION TIME**
**10 MINUTES COOKING TIME**

3 bunches of curly parsley
Salt and pepper
200 ml (7 fl oz) thin (pouring) cream
1.2 kg (2 lb 10 oz) skirt steak, membrane removed by the butcher
50 g (1¾ oz) butter, chopped
Sunflower oil, for frying
1 carrot, very finely diced
1 garlic clove, very finely diced

**THE PARSLEY PURÉE**

Dip 2 bunches of the parsley in a saucepan of boiling salted water for 10 seconds, refresh immediately in cold water and drain.

Heat the cream in a small saucepan over a medium–low heat for 2–3 minutes. Transfer to a food processor with the blanched parsley. Process to make a fairly coarse purée. Season.

**THE SKIRT STEAK**

Use a sharp knife to score the top of the skirt steak in a criss-cross pattern.

Heat the butter and 1 tablespoon of the sunflower oil in a large frying pan over a high heat. Cook the skirt steak, turning occasionally, with the diced carrot and garlic for 5–10 minutes (for very rare) or until cooked to desired level of doneness. Season. Transfer to a plate, cover with foil and rest for 10 minutes.

Pick the sprigs from the remaining bunch of parsley then deep-fry in sunflower oil until crisp. Remove to a paper towel to drain.

Serve the skirt steak with the juices from the pan, spoon a tablespoon of parsley purée over each serve and scatter over the fried parsley sprigs.

**SERVE WITH**

A potato purée with herbs.

# SKIRT STEAK PROVENÇAL

**SERVES 6**
**15 MINUTES PREPARATION TIME**
**15 MINUTES COOKING TIME**

- 1.2 kg (2 lb 10 oz) skirt steak, membrane removed by the butcher
- 100 g (3½ oz) butter, chopped
- 1 tablespoon sunflower oil
- 2½ tablespoons pastis (anise-flavoured liqueur)
- 200 ml (7 fl oz) veal stock
- 200 g (7 oz) sun-dried tomatoes in oil, drained and thinly sliced
- 200 g (7 oz) artichokes in oil, drained and sliced
- 50 g (1¾ oz) black dry-salted olives, pitted
- 4 garlic cloves, finely chopped
- 6 anchovies in oil, drained and chopped
- ½ a bunch of coriander (cilantro), finely chopped
- Salt and pepper

**PREPARATION**
Use a sharp knife to score the top of the skirt steak in a criss-cross pattern.

**COOKING**
Melt half of the butter with the sunflower oil in a large frying pan over a high heat. Add the steak and cook, turning occasionally, for 5–10 minutes (for very rare) or until cooked to the desired level of doneness. Season. Transfer to a plate, cover with foil and rest for 10 minutes.

**THE SAUCE**
Deglaze the frying pan with the pastis and reduce. Add the veal stock, sun-dried tomato, artichoke, olives, garlic and the anchovies. Cook, stirring occasionally, for 5 minutes. Add the coriander and remaining butter, and whisk together until the butter has melted.
Slice the meat, divide between the serving plates and spoon over the sauce and the vegetables. Let each individual season their own dish, as the olives and anchovies are already quite salty.

# MARROW BONES WITH CHIVES

**SERVES 6**
**5 MINUTES PREPARATION TIME**
**20 MINUTES COOKING TIME**

6 large marrow bones
Fine sea salt and cracked black pepper
1 bunch of chives, finely chopped
1 brioche bread loaf, sliced and toasted

**THE MARROW BONES**
Poach the marrow bones for 20 minutes in a large saucepan of boiling water. Set aside.

**THE BRIOCHE**
Sprinkle the bones with fine sea salt, pepper and chives. Eat everything with a spoon along with the brioche.

**SERVE WITH**
A good glass of Sancerre white.

# MARROW TOASTS

**SERVES 6**
**10 MINUTES PREPARATION TIME**
**25 MINUTES COOKING TIME**

6 large marrow bones
6 slices of good country-style bread
2 garlic cloves, halved lengthways
1 carrot, very finely diced
1 celery stalk, very thinly sliced
½ a bunch of chives, snipped
½ a bunch of chervil, leaves picked
Fine sea salt and cracked black pepper

**THE MARROW BONES**
Preheat the oven to 180°C (350°F/Gas 4).
Poach the marrow bones for 20 minutes in a large saucepan of boiling water. Set aside.

**THE TOASTS**
Meanwhile, rub the slices of bread with the garlic. Place on a baking tray and bake until the bread is golden brown. Spread the bread with the marrow scooped from inside the bone and sprinkle over the carrot, celery, chives and chervil. Season and serve immediately.

# SPINAL CORD WITH OYSTER MUSHROOMS

**SERVES 6**
**15 MINUTES PREPARATION TIME**
**25 MINUTES COOKING TIME**

- 50 g (1¾ oz) butter, chopped
- 1 tablespoon sunflower oil
- 2 garlic cloves, peeled
- 4 French shallots, peeled and halved lengthways
- 600 g (1 lb 5 oz) oyster mushrooms, thickly sliced
- 50 g (1¾ oz/⅓ cup) plain (all-purpose) flour
- 600 g (1 lb 5 oz) lamb's spinal cord
- Salt and pepper
- 2 tablespoons raspberry vinegar
- ¼ bunch of flat-leaf (Italian) parsley, leaves picked

**THE MUSHROOMS**

Melt the butter with the sunflower oil in a large frying pan over a medium–low heat. Slowly cook the garlic cloves and shallots, stirring occasionally, for 10 minutes.
Add the mushrooms and cook, stirring occasionally, for a further 5 minutes. Transfer the mixture to a plate and cover to keep warm.

**THE SPINAL CORD**

Place the flour in a shallow bowl. Dust the spinal cord in flour and shake off any excess. Add to the frying pan and cook over a medium–high heat for 5 minutes or until browned all over. Return the mushroom mixture to the pan. Season then deglaze with the raspberry vinegar. Serve as a starter, adding the parsley at the last moment.

# LES TESTICULES

## UDDERS & TESTICLES

**CALF, PIG OR LAMB TESTICLES**
lamb 'fries' can be ordered ahead of time from specialty butchers ready to cook

## UDDERS ARE THE MAMMARY GLANDS OF MAMMALS

## FRIES ARE TESTICLES, SPECIFICALLY OF LAMBS

We were always going to need some X-rated material to fuel our fantasies of an uninhibited and hedonistic cuisine. A real cuisine, in other words! Because yes, food has to be generous like the kiss of lovers reuniting, and sensual like a caress of the small of the back. It should provide all the emotion of the first time, offer pleasure with each mouthful, elicit ecstasy. Cooking brings all the senses to the fore. Once the sensory realm has conquered the intellectual one, TKO orgasm is never far away. Teats and testicles together form the end point of our fantasies. Here, they are cooked for other pleasures.

# COW UDDER WITH SAUCE GRIBICHE

**SERVES 6**
**15 MINUTES PREPARATION TIME**
**20 MINUTES COOKING TIME**

1 pre-cooked cow udder (see note)
50 g (1¾ oz/⅓ cup) plain (all-purpose) flour
Salt and pepper
100 ml (3½ fl oz) sunflower oil
2 eggs, hard-boiled
1 tablespoon dijon mustard
1 teaspoon lemon juice
1 teaspoon white wine vinegar
150 ml (5½ fl oz) olive oil
1 tablespoon capers, rinsed
1 French shallot, finely chopped
200 g (7 oz) mâche lettuce (lamb's lettuce)

**THE UDDER**

Cut the udder into thick slices. Place the flour in a shallow bowl and season. Dust the slices of udder in flour to completely cover, shaking off any excess.

**COOKING**

Heat the sunflower oil in a large frying pan over a medium–high heat then brown the slices of udder, in batches, for 5 minutes on each side until golden. Set aside on paper towels to drain.

**THE SAUCE**

Mash the egg yolks with the mustard then add the lemon juice and vinegar. Whisk, adding 100 ml (3½ fl oz) of the olive oil. Mix in the capers, shallot and roughly mashed egg whites.

Dress the mâche lettuce with the rest of the olive oil and serve the udder, topped with some lettuce and sauce gribiche drizzled over.

**NOTE**

Alas! Not all countries embrace the pale, gentle wonders of the udder. If you live in a country where the butcher's stocks are *sans udder*, serve this sauce gribiche with other meats (such as calf's head). Or, better yet, tear out this page and take it with you on your travels. You never know when a trip to France or other udder-loving locale may beckon…

# LAMB FRIES WITH PEPPER

**SERVES 6**
**15 MINUTES PREPARATION TIME**
**15 MINUTES COOKING TIME**

12 g (⅖ oz) lamb fries (testicles), prepared by the butcher (see note)
50 g (1¾ oz) butter
1 tablespoon sunflower oil
3 garlic cloves, finely chopped
4 bulb spring onions (scallions), thinly sliced
200 ml (7 fl oz) white port
Salt and cracked black pepper

**PREPARATION**
Remove any outer membranes from the lamb fries then cut each one in half.

**COOKING**
Melt the butter and sunflower oil in a medium frying pan over a medium–high heat. Sauté the lamb fries with the garlic and spring onion for 5 minutes, stirring occasionally, until browned. Deglaze with the port then reduce until all the liquid has evaporated. Season and serve immediately.

**HOW SHOULD I SERVE THEM?**
As an aperitif, to give everyone a surprise.

**NOTE**
Lamb fries (definitely not to be confused with 'lamb's fry', which is what a lamb's liver is called in certain countries, such as Australia) can be purchased from specialty butchers but will need to be ordered ahead of time.

ABCDE
FGHIJK
LMNOP
QRSTU
VWXYZ

# TABLE DES MATIÈRES
# LIST OF RECIPES

# THE OFFAL COUNTER

| | ANIMAL | FAMILY | WEIGHT | SOLD | APPEARANCE |
|---|---|---|---|---|---|
| **LIVER** | COW | RED | 5 to 7 kg (11 to 16 lb 8 oz) | BY THE SLICE | DARK RED |
| | CALF | | 2 to 3 kg (4 lb 8 oz to 6 lb 12 oz) | | BLOND[1] |
| | PIG | | 600 to 800 g (1 lb 5 oz to 1 lb 12 oz) | BY WEIGHT | DARK RED |
| | POULTRY | | 30 to 50 g (1 to 1¾ oz) | | BLOND[1] |
| **KIDNEY** | BEEF | RED | 300 to 500 g (10½ to 1 lb 2 oz) | WHOLE | DARK RED |
| | CALF | | 250 to 400 g (9 to 14 oz) | | LIGHT BROWN |
| | LAMB | | 60 to 80 g (2¼ to 2¾ oz) | | |
| | PIG | | 120 to 180 g (4¼ to 6⅛ oz) | | DARK RED |
| **TRIPE** | BEEF | WHITE | 1 to 3 kg (2 lb 4 to 6 lb 12 oz) | BY WEIGHT | CREAM |
| **GIZZARD** | POULTRY | RED | 15 to 30 g (½ to 1 oz) | BY WEIGHT | DARK BROWN |
| **SWEETBREAD** | CALF | WHITE | 400 to 500 g (14 oz to 1 lb 2 oz) | BY WEIGHT | CREAMY WHITE |
| | LAMB | | 80 to 120 g (2¾ to 4¼ oz) | | |
| **HEART** | BEEF | RED | 250 to 300 g (9 to 10½ oz) | BY WEIGHT | UNIFORM RED |
| | CALF | | 150 to 200 g (5½ to 7 oz) | WHOLE | |
| | LAMB | | 100 to 150 g (3½ to 5½ oz) | | |
| | DUCK | | 20 g (¾ oz) | | |
| **FOOT** | CALF | WHITE | 800 g to 1.2 kg (1 lb 12 to 2 lb 10 oz) | BY THE PIECE | CREAMY WHITE |
| | LAMB | | 100 to 200 g (3½ to 7 oz) | | |
| | PIG | | 300 to 500 g (10½ to 1 lb 2 oz) | | PINK |
| **TAIL** | BEEF | RED | 900 g to 1.2 kg (2 lb to 2 lb 10 oz) | BY THE PIECE | DARK RED |
| | PIG | | 150 to 200 g (5½ to 7 oz) | | CREAMY WHITE |
| **CHEEK** | BEEF | RED | 600 to 700 g (1 lb 5 to 1 lb 9 oz) | BY WEIGHT | DARK RED |
| | PIG | | 80 to 100 g (2¾ to 3¾ oz) | | PINK |
| **TONGUE** | BEEF | RED | 1.2 to 1.5 kg (2 lb 10 to 3 lb 5 oz) | BY THE PIECE | PINK |
| | CALF | | 700 g to 1 kg (1 lb 9 to 2 lb 4 oz) | | |
| | LAMB | | 120 to 150 g (4¼ to 5½ oz) | | |
| | PIG | | 120 to 150 g (4¼ to 5½ oz) | | |
| **BRAINS** | CALF | WHITE | 200 to 250 g (7 to 9 oz) | BY THE PIECE | PALE, SLIGHTLY VEINED |
| | LAMB | | 80 to 100 g (2¾ to 3¾ oz) | | |
| | PIG | | 150 to 180 g (5½ to 6⅛ oz) | | |
| **HEAD** | CALF | WHITE | 1.5 to 2.5 kg (for a rolled half head) (3 lb 5 to 5 lb 8 oz) | BY THE PIECE OR BY WEIGHT | LARGE SAUSAGE WRAPPED IN FISHNET MESH |
| | PIG | WHITE | 3 to 5 kg (6 lb 12 oz to 11 lb) | WHOLE, SNOUT AND EARS BY THE PIECE | PALE |
| **SPINAL CORD** | LAMB | WHITE | 100 g (3½ oz) | BY WEIGHT | PALE PINK – WHITE |
| **TESTICLES** | LAMB/SHEEP | WHITE | 80 g (2¾ oz) | BY THE PIECE | CREAMY WHITE |
| **UDDER** | COW | WHITE | 400 to 600 g (14 to 1 lb 5 oz) | BY THE PIECE | PINK |

# BUTCHER'S CUTS

| | ANIMAL | FAMILY | WEIGHT | SOLD | APPEARANCE |
|---|---|---|---|---|---|
| **HANGER STEAK** | BEEF | RED | 500 to 800 g (1 lb 2 to 1 lb 12 oz) | BY WEIGHT | DARK RED |
| **SKIRT STEAK** | BEEF | RED | 500 to 800 g (1 lb 2 to 1 lb 12 oz) | BY WEIGHT | DARK RED |
| **POPE'S EYE (SPIDER STEAK)** | BEEF | RED | 400 to 600 g (14 to 1 lb 5 oz) | BY WEIGHT | DARK RED |
| **MARROW BONE** | BEEF | - | DEPENDING ON THE SIZE OF THE BONES | BY WEIGHT, BY THE CUT, BY THE PIECE | SLIGHTLY PINK |